50 Israeli Dinner Recipes for Home

By: Kelly Johnson

Table of Contents

- Shakshuka
- Falafel with tahini sauce
- Hummus with pita bread
- Israeli couscous salad
- Chicken shawarma
- Sabich (Israeli sandwich)
- Beef kebabs with grilled vegetables
- Stuffed grape leaves (Dolmas)
- Tahini chicken with roasted vegetables
- Israeli-style grilled fish
- Eggplant schnitzel
- Lamb kofta
- Matzo ball soup
- Mujadara (Lentils and rice)
- Schnitzel with lemon sauce
- Israeli chopped salad
- Bourekas (pastry filled with cheese or spinach)
- Stuffed peppers with rice and beef
- Moroccan fish tagine
- Israeli-style stuffed chicken breast
- Spinach and cheese burekas
- Kebab in pita with tahini sauce
- Potato latkes
- Grilled halloumi cheese with honey
- Israeli vegetable tagine
- Lemon herb roasted chicken
- Israeli-style meatballs in tomato sauce
- Grilled lamb chops with mint sauce
- Falafel burger
- Chicken schnitzel sandwich
- Shakshuka with feta cheese
- Sabich bowl (deconstructed sabich)
- Jerusalem mixed grill
- Tabbouleh salad
- Shawarma bowl with rice and tahini sauce

- Stuffed eggplant with lamb and pine nuts
- Spinach and feta borekas
- Israeli beef stew with potatoes and carrots
- Grilled za'atar chicken skewers
- Mediterranean stuffed zucchini
- Spiced lamb burgers with yogurt sauce
- Herb-crusted salmon
- Israeli-style ratatouille
- Harissa roasted vegetables
- Beef and eggplant moussaka
- Chicken and vegetable kebabs with sumac
- Lamb shawarma bowl
- Spicy tomato and pepper soup
- Baked falafel with tahini dressing
- Israeli-style stuffed cabbage rolls

Shakshuka

Ingredients:

- 2 tablespoons olive oil
- 1 onion, chopped
- 2 bell peppers (red, yellow, or orange), diced
- 3 cloves garlic, minced
- 1 teaspoon ground cumin
- 1 teaspoon smoked paprika
- 1/2 teaspoon chili flakes (adjust to taste)
- 1 can (14 ounces) diced tomatoes
- Salt and pepper to taste
- 4-6 large eggs
- Fresh parsley or cilantro, chopped (for garnish)
- Crumbled feta cheese (optional, for garnish)
- Crusty bread or pita, for serving

Instructions:

1. Heat the olive oil in a large skillet or frying pan over medium heat.
2. Add the chopped onion and diced bell peppers to the skillet. Cook until softened, about 5-7 minutes.
3. Stir in the minced garlic, ground cumin, smoked paprika, and chili flakes. Cook for another 1-2 minutes until fragrant.
4. Pour in the diced tomatoes with their juices. Season with salt and pepper to taste. Stir well to combine all the ingredients.
5. Reduce the heat to medium-low and let the sauce simmer for about 10-15 minutes, stirring occasionally, until it thickens slightly.
6. Using a spoon, create small wells in the sauce for the eggs. Crack the eggs directly into the wells.
7. Cover the skillet with a lid and let the eggs cook in the sauce until the whites are set but the yolks are still runny, about 5-7 minutes. If you prefer firmer yolks, cook for a few minutes longer.
8. Once the eggs are cooked to your liking, remove the skillet from the heat. Garnish with chopped parsley or cilantro and crumbled feta cheese, if desired.

9. Serve the Shakshuka hot straight from the skillet with crusty bread or pita for dipping.

Enjoy your delicious homemade Shakshuka!

Falafel with tahini sauce

Ingredients:

- 1 cup dried chickpeas, soaked overnight
- 1 small onion, roughly chopped
- 3 cloves garlic, minced
- 1/4 cup fresh parsley, chopped
- 1/4 cup fresh cilantro, chopped
- 1 teaspoon ground cumin
- 1 teaspoon ground coriander
- 1/4 teaspoon cayenne pepper (optional)
- 1 teaspoon salt, or to taste
- 1/2 teaspoon baking soda
- 2 tablespoons all-purpose flour or chickpea flour (for gluten-free option)
- Vegetable oil for frying

Instructions:

1. Drain the soaked chickpeas and rinse them thoroughly. Pat them dry with a clean kitchen towel or paper towels.
2. In a food processor, combine the chickpeas, onion, garlic, parsley, cilantro, cumin, coriander, cayenne pepper (if using), salt, and baking soda. Pulse the mixture until it becomes a coarse paste, scraping down the sides of the bowl as needed.
3. Transfer the falafel mixture to a bowl and stir in the flour until well combined. The mixture should hold together when shaped into balls.
4. With damp hands, shape the falafel mixture into small balls or patties, about 1 1/2 inches in diameter.
5. Heat vegetable oil in a deep frying pan or pot to 350°F (175°C). Carefully add the falafel balls/patties to the hot oil in batches, making sure not to overcrowd the pan.
6. Fry the falafel until they are golden brown and crispy on the outside, about 3-4 minutes per side. Use a slotted spoon to transfer the cooked falafel to a plate lined with paper towels to drain excess oil.
7. Serve the falafel hot with tahini sauce, pita bread, and your favorite toppings.

Tahini Sauce:

Ingredients:

- 1/2 cup tahini paste
- 1/4 cup water
- 2 tablespoons lemon juice
- 2 cloves garlic, minced
- Salt to taste

Instructions:

1. In a small bowl, whisk together the tahini paste, water, lemon juice, minced garlic, and salt until smooth and creamy. Adjust the consistency by adding more water if needed.
2. Taste the tahini sauce and adjust the seasoning according to your preference, adding more salt or lemon juice if desired.
3. Serve the tahini sauce alongside the falafel for dipping or drizzle it over the falafel before serving.

Enjoy your homemade falafel with creamy tahini sauce!

Hummus with pita bread

Ingredients:

- 1 can (15 ounces) chickpeas (garbanzo beans), drained and rinsed
- 1/4 cup tahini paste
- 2 tablespoons lemon juice (about 1 lemon)
- 2 cloves garlic, minced
- 2 tablespoons extra virgin olive oil, plus more for serving
- 1/2 teaspoon ground cumin
- Salt to taste
- 2-4 tablespoons water (optional, for desired consistency)
- Paprika and chopped fresh parsley for garnish (optional)

Instructions:

1. In a food processor, combine the chickpeas, tahini paste, lemon juice, minced garlic, olive oil, ground cumin, and a pinch of salt.
2. Blend the ingredients until smooth and creamy, scraping down the sides of the bowl as needed. If the hummus is too thick, you can add 2-4 tablespoons of water, one tablespoon at a time, until you reach your desired consistency.
3. Taste the hummus and adjust the seasoning, adding more salt or lemon juice if needed.
4. Transfer the hummus to a serving bowl. Drizzle a little extra virgin olive oil over the top and sprinkle with paprika and chopped fresh parsley for garnish, if desired.
5. Serve the hummus at room temperature or chilled, alongside warm pita bread for dipping.

Pita Bread:

Ingredients:

- Store-bought or homemade pita bread

Instructions:

1. If using store-bought pita bread, you can warm it in the oven or microwave according to the package instructions.
2. If making homemade pita bread, you can find recipes online or use your favorite recipe. Homemade pita bread is typically baked in a hot oven until it puffs up and becomes slightly golden brown.

Serving:

1. Cut the warm pita bread into triangles or tear it into pieces.
2. Arrange the pita bread pieces around the bowl of hummus.
3. Dip the warm pita bread into the creamy hummus and enjoy!

You can also serve hummus with a variety of toppings such as olive oil, olives, chopped tomatoes, cucumbers, roasted red peppers, or pine nuts for added flavor and texture. Experiment with different combinations to find your favorite way to enjoy hummus and pita bread!

Israeli couscous salad

Ingredients:

- 1 cup Israeli couscous
- 1 1/4 cups water or vegetable broth
- 1 tablespoon olive oil
- 1 cup cherry tomatoes, halved
- 1/2 English cucumber, diced
- 1/4 red onion, finely chopped
- 1/4 cup Kalamata olives, sliced
- 2 tablespoons fresh parsley, chopped
- 2 tablespoons fresh mint, chopped
- 2 tablespoons lemon juice
- 2 tablespoons extra virgin olive oil
- Salt and pepper to taste
- Crumbled feta cheese (optional, for garnish)

Instructions:

1. In a medium saucepan, heat 1 tablespoon of olive oil over medium heat. Add the Israeli couscous and toast it, stirring frequently, until it turns golden brown, about 3-4 minutes.
2. Pour in the water or vegetable broth and bring it to a boil. Reduce the heat to low, cover the saucepan, and simmer for 10-12 minutes, or until the couscous is tender and has absorbed all the liquid. Remove from heat and let it cool slightly.
3. In a large mixing bowl, combine the cooked Israeli couscous, halved cherry tomatoes, diced cucumber, finely chopped red onion, sliced Kalamata olives, chopped parsley, and chopped mint.
4. In a small bowl, whisk together the lemon juice, extra virgin olive oil, salt, and pepper to make the dressing.
5. Pour the dressing over the couscous salad and toss until all the ingredients are well coated.
6. Taste the salad and adjust the seasoning if needed, adding more salt, pepper, or lemon juice according to your preference.
7. Transfer the Israeli couscous salad to a serving platter or bowl. If desired, garnish with crumbled feta cheese for extra flavor.
8. Serve the salad at room temperature or chilled, as a side dish or a light meal.

Enjoy this delicious and vibrant Israeli couscous salad! Feel free to customize it with your favorite vegetables, herbs, or additional toppings like toasted pine nuts or diced avocado.

Chicken shawarma

Ingredients:

For the marinade:

- 1.5 lbs (about 700g) boneless, skinless chicken thighs or breasts, thinly sliced
- 1/4 cup plain yogurt
- 3 tablespoons olive oil
- 3 cloves garlic, minced
- 2 tablespoons lemon juice
- 1 tablespoon ground cumin
- 1 tablespoon ground coriander
- 1 teaspoon paprika
- 1 teaspoon turmeric
- 1/2 teaspoon ground cinnamon
- 1/2 teaspoon ground cloves
- Salt and black pepper to taste

For serving:

- Pita bread or flatbread
- Sliced tomatoes
- Sliced cucumbers
- Sliced onions
- Chopped parsley or cilantro
- Tahini sauce or garlic sauce (optional)

Instructions:

1. In a large mixing bowl, combine all the marinade ingredients: yogurt, olive oil, minced garlic, lemon juice, ground cumin, ground coriander, paprika, turmeric, cinnamon, cloves, salt, and black pepper. Mix until well combined.
2. Add the thinly sliced chicken to the marinade, ensuring that each piece is coated evenly. Cover the bowl and refrigerate for at least 1 hour, or preferably overnight, to allow the flavors to develop.

3. Preheat your grill or grill pan over medium-high heat. If using a grill pan, you may need to lightly oil it to prevent sticking.
4. Thread the marinated chicken slices onto skewers, or place them directly on the grill grates. Cook for 4-5 minutes on each side, or until the chicken is cooked through and slightly charred.
5. Once cooked, remove the chicken from the grill and let it rest for a few minutes. Then, use a sharp knife to thinly slice the chicken into strips.
6. To serve, warm the pita bread or flatbread. Place a generous amount of sliced chicken onto each piece of bread, along with sliced tomatoes, cucumbers, onions, and chopped parsley or cilantro.
7. Drizzle with tahini sauce or garlic sauce, if desired.
8. Fold the pita bread over the filling to form a sandwich or roll it up like a wrap.
9. Serve the chicken shawarma immediately, and enjoy!

Feel free to customize your chicken shawarma with your favorite toppings and sauces.

This recipe also works well with beef or lamb if you prefer.

Sabich (Israeli sandwich)

Ingredients:

- 4 pita bread rounds
- 1 large eggplant, thinly sliced
- 4 hard-boiled eggs, sliced
- 1 cup Israeli salad (diced tomatoes, cucumbers, and onions)
- 1/2 cup hummus
- 1/2 cup tahini sauce
- 1/4 cup amba (pickled mango sauce)
- Vegetable oil for frying
- Salt and pepper to taste
- Fresh parsley or cilantro for garnish (optional)

Instructions:

1. Heat vegetable oil in a large skillet or frying pan over medium heat. Once the oil is hot, add the thinly sliced eggplant in batches and fry until golden brown and crispy on both sides. Transfer the fried eggplant slices to a plate lined with paper towels to drain excess oil. Season with salt and pepper to taste.
2. Warm the pita bread rounds in the oven or on a dry skillet until they are soft and pliable.
3. To assemble each Sabich sandwich, spread a generous spoonful of hummus on one side of the warm pita bread.
4. Layer the fried eggplant slices, sliced hard-boiled eggs, Israeli salad, and drizzle with tahini sauce and amba (pickled mango sauce).
5. Garnish with fresh parsley or cilantro, if desired.
6. Fold the pita bread over the filling to form a sandwich or roll it up like a wrap.
7. Serve the Sabich sandwiches immediately, while still warm.

Enjoy the delicious combination of flavors and textures in this classic Israeli sandwich!

Feel free to adjust the ingredients and quantities according to your preference.

Beef kebabs with grilled vegetables

Ingredients:

For the beef kebabs:

- 1.5 lbs (about 700g) beef sirloin or tenderloin, cut into 1-inch cubes
- 1/4 cup olive oil
- 3 cloves garlic, minced
- 2 tablespoons soy sauce
- 1 tablespoon Worcestershire sauce
- 1 tablespoon lemon juice
- 1 teaspoon paprika
- 1 teaspoon ground cumin
- 1 teaspoon dried oregano
- Salt and black pepper to taste
- Wooden or metal skewers

For the grilled vegetables:

- Assorted vegetables such as bell peppers, zucchini, onions, and cherry tomatoes, cut into bite-sized pieces
- Olive oil for brushing
- Salt and black pepper to taste
- Optional: fresh herbs such as rosemary or thyme for extra flavor

Instructions:

1. In a large bowl, combine the olive oil, minced garlic, soy sauce, Worcestershire sauce, lemon juice, paprika, ground cumin, dried oregano, salt, and black pepper to make the marinade for the beef kebabs.
2. Add the cubed beef to the marinade and toss until well coated. Cover the bowl and refrigerate for at least 30 minutes, or preferably 2-4 hours, to allow the flavors to meld.
3. If using wooden skewers, soak them in water for at least 30 minutes to prevent them from burning on the grill.

4. Preheat your grill to medium-high heat.
5. Thread the marinated beef cubes onto skewers, leaving a little space between each piece.
6. Prepare the vegetables by tossing them with olive oil, salt, and black pepper in a separate bowl.
7. Thread the seasoned vegetables onto skewers, alternating with the beef kebabs.
8. If desired, sprinkle the vegetable skewers with fresh herbs for extra flavor.
9. Place the beef kebabs and vegetable skewers on the preheated grill. Cook for 8-10 minutes, turning occasionally, or until the beef is cooked to your desired level of doneness and the vegetables are tender and slightly charred.
10. Once cooked, remove the kebabs from the grill and let them rest for a few minutes.
11. Serve the beef kebabs and grilled vegetables hot, garnished with additional fresh herbs if desired.

Enjoy the juicy and flavorful beef kebabs alongside the smoky grilled vegetables for a delicious meal! You can also serve them with rice, couscous, or a salad for a complete and satisfying dish.

Stuffed grape leaves (Dolmas)

Ingredients:

- 1 jar of grape leaves in brine (about 50 leaves), or fresh grape leaves if available
- 1 cup long-grain white rice
- 1/2 lb ground beef or lamb (optional)
- 1 large onion, finely chopped
- 2 cloves garlic, minced
- 1/4 cup fresh dill, chopped
- 1/4 cup fresh mint, chopped
- 1/4 cup fresh parsley, chopped
- 1/4 cup pine nuts, toasted (optional)
- 1/4 cup raisins (optional)
- 2 tablespoons olive oil
- Juice of 1 lemon
- Salt and pepper to taste
- Water or chicken broth

Instructions:

1. If using grape leaves from a jar, rinse them under cold water to remove excess salt, then drain and pat dry with paper towels. If using fresh grape leaves, blanch them in boiling water for about 30 seconds, then drain and rinse under cold water.
2. In a large mixing bowl, combine the rice, ground beef or lamb (if using), chopped onion, minced garlic, chopped dill, chopped mint, chopped parsley, toasted pine nuts (if using), raisins (if using), olive oil, lemon juice, salt, and pepper. Mix well to combine all the ingredients.
3. Place a grape leaf flat on a clean work surface, shiny side down, with the stem facing towards you.
4. Spoon a small amount of the rice mixture (about 1 tablespoon) onto the center of the grape leaf, near the stem.
5. Fold the bottom of the grape leaf over the filling, then fold the sides towards the center, and roll it up tightly into a cigar shape.

6. Repeat the process with the remaining grape leaves and rice mixture, placing the stuffed grape leaves seam side down in a large pot or Dutch oven, arranging them snugly in a single layer.
7. Once all the grape leaves are stuffed and arranged in the pot, pour enough water or chicken broth over them to just cover them.
8. Place a heatproof plate upside down on top of the grape leaves to weigh them down and prevent them from unraveling during cooking.
9. Cover the pot with a lid and bring the liquid to a gentle simmer over medium heat.
10. Reduce the heat to low and let the stuffed grape leaves simmer gently for about 45-60 minutes, or until the rice is cooked through and the grape leaves are tender.
11. Once cooked, remove the stuffed grape leaves from the pot using a slotted spoon and transfer them to a serving platter.
12. Serve the stuffed grape leaves warm or at room temperature, garnished with lemon wedges and additional fresh herbs if desired.

Enjoy the delicious and flavorful stuffed grape leaves as a appetizer or part of a mezze spread! They can also be served as a main dish with yogurt or tzatziki sauce on the side.

Tahini chicken with roasted vegetables

Ingredients:

For the tahini chicken:

- 4 boneless, skinless chicken breasts
- 1/4 cup tahini paste
- 2 tablespoons olive oil
- 2 cloves garlic, minced
- 2 tablespoons lemon juice
- 1 teaspoon ground cumin
- 1 teaspoon paprika
- Salt and pepper to taste
- Fresh parsley or cilantro for garnish (optional)

For the roasted vegetables:

- 2 large carrots, peeled and cut into sticks
- 2 bell peppers, seeded and sliced
- 1 large red onion, sliced
- 1 small eggplant, diced
- 2 tablespoons olive oil
- 1 teaspoon ground cumin
- 1 teaspoon paprika
- Salt and pepper to taste

Instructions:

1. Preheat your oven to 400°F (200°C) and line a baking sheet with parchment paper or aluminum foil.
2. In a small bowl, whisk together the tahini paste, olive oil, minced garlic, lemon juice, ground cumin, paprika, salt, and pepper to make the marinade for the chicken.
3. Place the chicken breasts in a shallow dish or resealable plastic bag, and pour the tahini marinade over them. Make sure the chicken is evenly coated with the

marinade. Cover and refrigerate for at least 30 minutes, or preferably 2-4 hours, to allow the flavors to meld.
4. In a separate large mixing bowl, toss together the sliced carrots, bell peppers, sliced red onion, and diced eggplant with olive oil, ground cumin, paprika, salt, and pepper until evenly coated.
5. Spread the seasoned vegetables in a single layer on the prepared baking sheet.
6. Remove the marinated chicken breasts from the refrigerator and place them on the baking sheet with the vegetables.
7. Roast in the preheated oven for 20-25 minutes, or until the chicken is cooked through and the vegetables are tender and slightly caramelized, stirring the vegetables halfway through cooking.
8. Once cooked, remove the baking sheet from the oven and let the chicken rest for a few minutes before slicing.
9. Serve the tahini chicken with roasted vegetables hot, garnished with fresh parsley or cilantro if desired.

Enjoy this flavorful and satisfying tahini chicken with roasted vegetables as a wholesome meal! It's perfect for a family dinner or for meal prep for the week ahead.

Israeli-style grilled fish

Ingredients:

- 4 fish fillets (such as sea bass, tilapia, or trout)
- 2 tablespoons olive oil
- 2 cloves garlic, minced
- 2 tablespoons fresh lemon juice
- 1 teaspoon paprika
- 1 teaspoon ground cumin
- 1 teaspoon ground coriander
- 1/2 teaspoon turmeric
- Salt and black pepper to taste
- Lemon wedges for serving
- Fresh parsley for garnish (optional)

Instructions:

1. Preheat your grill to medium-high heat. If using a charcoal grill, wait until the coals are hot and white.
2. In a small bowl, whisk together the olive oil, minced garlic, fresh lemon juice, paprika, ground cumin, ground coriander, turmeric, salt, and black pepper to make the marinade for the fish.
3. Pat the fish fillets dry with paper towels and place them in a shallow dish or resealable plastic bag.
4. Pour the marinade over the fish fillets, making sure they are evenly coated. Cover and refrigerate for at least 30 minutes, or preferably 1-2 hours, to allow the flavors to develop.
5. Remove the fish fillets from the marinade and discard any excess marinade.
6. Lightly oil the grill grates to prevent the fish from sticking. Place the fish fillets on the preheated grill.
7. Grill the fish for 3-4 minutes per side, or until they are cooked through and have grill marks on both sides. The cooking time will depend on the thickness of the fish fillets.
8. Once cooked, transfer the grilled fish to a serving platter.
9. Garnish the grilled fish with fresh parsley and serve hot, accompanied by lemon wedges for squeezing over the fish.

Enjoy the tender and flavorful Israeli-style grilled fish as a main dish, served with your favorite side dishes such as grilled vegetables, rice, or a fresh salad. It's a perfect dish for a summer barbecue or a weeknight dinner with family and friends.

Eggplant schnitzel

Ingredients:

- 2 large eggplants
- 2 eggs
- 1/2 cup all-purpose flour
- 1 cup breadcrumbs
- 1/2 cup grated Parmesan cheese (optional)
- 1 teaspoon garlic powder
- 1 teaspoon paprika
- Salt and pepper to taste
- Vegetable oil for frying
- Lemon wedges for serving
- Fresh parsley for garnish (optional)

Instructions:

1. Slice the eggplants into rounds, about 1/2 inch thick. Sprinkle the eggplant slices with salt and let them sit for 15-20 minutes to draw out excess moisture. Pat the slices dry with paper towels.
2. Prepare three shallow bowls or plates: one with the flour, one with beaten eggs, and one with a mixture of breadcrumbs, grated Parmesan cheese (if using), garlic powder, paprika, salt, and pepper.
3. Dredge each eggplant slice in the flour, shaking off any excess. Then dip it into the beaten eggs, allowing any excess to drip off. Finally, coat it evenly in the breadcrumb mixture, pressing gently to adhere.
4. Heat vegetable oil in a large skillet or frying pan over medium heat. Once the oil is hot, add the breaded eggplant slices in batches, making sure not to overcrowd the pan.
5. Fry the eggplant slices for 3-4 minutes on each side, or until golden brown and crispy. Use a spatula to carefully flip them halfway through cooking.
6. Once cooked, transfer the fried eggplant schnitzel to a plate lined with paper towels to drain excess oil.
7. Repeat the process with the remaining eggplant slices, adding more oil to the pan if needed.

8. Serve the eggplant schnitzel hot, garnished with fresh parsley and lemon wedges for squeezing over the top.

Enjoy the crispy and flavorful eggplant schnitzel as a main dish, served with a side salad, mashed potatoes, or your favorite dipping sauce. It's a satisfying and comforting meal that's sure to please vegetarians and meat-lovers alike!

Lamb kofta

Ingredients:

- 1 lb ground lamb
- 1 small onion, finely chopped
- 2 cloves garlic, minced
- 1/4 cup fresh parsley, chopped
- 1/4 cup fresh cilantro, chopped
- 1 teaspoon ground cumin
- 1 teaspoon ground coriander
- 1/2 teaspoon paprika
- 1/2 teaspoon ground cinnamon
- 1/4 teaspoon ground nutmeg
- 1/4 teaspoon cayenne pepper (optional, for heat)
- Salt and black pepper to taste
- Olive oil for grilling or frying
- Skewers (if making kebabs)

Instructions:

1. In a large mixing bowl, combine the ground lamb, chopped onion, minced garlic, chopped parsley, chopped cilantro, ground cumin, ground coriander, paprika, ground cinnamon, ground nutmeg, cayenne pepper (if using), salt, and black pepper. Mix until all the ingredients are well combined.
2. If making patties: Divide the lamb mixture into equal portions and shape each portion into small oval-shaped patties, about 2-3 inches long and 1 inch thick.
3. If making kebabs: Pre-soak wooden skewers in water for at least 30 minutes to prevent them from burning. Take a portion of the lamb mixture and mold it around the skewer, forming a long sausage shape. Repeat with the remaining lamb mixture.
4. Preheat your grill to medium-high heat. If using a grill pan or skillet, heat it over medium-high heat on the stovetop.
5. Brush the grill grates or skillet with olive oil to prevent sticking.
6. Place the lamb kofta patties or skewers on the preheated grill or skillet. Cook for 4-5 minutes on each side, or until they are cooked through and have a nice charred exterior.

7. Once cooked, remove the lamb kofta from the grill or skillet and let them rest for a few minutes before serving.
8. Serve the lamb kofta hot, garnished with additional fresh herbs if desired. You can also serve them with pita bread, tzatziki sauce, hummus, or a fresh salad.

Enjoy the flavorful and juicy lamb kofta as a main dish or part of a Middle Eastern-inspired feast!

Matzo ball soup

Ingredients:

For the matzo balls:

- 4 large eggs
- 1/4 cup vegetable oil or schmaltz (rendered chicken fat)
- 1 cup matzo meal
- 1/4 cup seltzer water or chicken broth
- 1 teaspoon salt
- 1/4 teaspoon black pepper
- 1/4 teaspoon garlic powder (optional)
- 1/4 teaspoon onion powder (optional)
- Chopped fresh dill or parsley for garnish (optional)

For the soup:

- 8 cups chicken broth (homemade or store-bought)
- 2 carrots, peeled and sliced
- 2 celery stalks, sliced
- 1 onion, diced
- 2 cloves garlic, minced
- 1 parsnip, peeled and sliced (optional)
- Salt and pepper to taste
- Chopped fresh dill or parsley for garnish (optional)

Instructions:

1. In a large mixing bowl, beat the eggs until well combined.
2. Gradually add the vegetable oil or schmaltz to the beaten eggs, whisking continuously until fully incorporated.
3. Stir in the matzo meal, seltzer water or chicken broth, salt, black pepper, garlic powder (if using), and onion powder (if using) until a thick batter forms. Cover the bowl and refrigerate for at least 30 minutes, or up to 2 hours, to allow the mixture to firm up.

4. While the matzo ball mixture is chilling, prepare the soup. In a large pot, bring the chicken broth to a simmer over medium heat.
5. Add the sliced carrots, celery, diced onion, minced garlic, and sliced parsnip (if using) to the pot. Season with salt and pepper to taste.
6. Simmer the soup, uncovered, for about 15-20 minutes, or until the vegetables are tender.
7. After the matzo ball mixture has chilled, bring a large pot of salted water to a boil.
8. With damp hands, shape the chilled matzo ball mixture into small balls, about 1 inch in diameter. Drop the matzo balls into the boiling water.
9. Reduce the heat to low, cover the pot, and simmer the matzo balls for about 20-25 minutes, or until they are cooked through and tender. They will float to the surface when done.
10. Using a slotted spoon, carefully transfer the cooked matzo balls from the boiling water to the pot of simmering soup.
11. Let the matzo balls simmer in the soup for an additional 5 minutes to absorb the flavors.
12. Ladle the hot matzo ball soup into serving bowls. Garnish with chopped fresh dill or parsley if desired.

Enjoy the comforting and nourishing matzo ball soup as a starter or a light meal, especially during cold weather or when you're feeling under the weather.

Mujadara (Lentils and rice)

Ingredients:

- 1 cup brown or green lentils, rinsed and drained
- 1 cup white rice (long-grain or basmati)
- 2 large onions, thinly sliced
- 4 tablespoons olive oil
- 4 cups vegetable broth or water
- 1 teaspoon ground cumin
- 1 teaspoon ground coriander
- 1/2 teaspoon ground cinnamon
- Salt and pepper to taste
- Fresh parsley or cilantro for garnish (optional)
- Yogurt or tahini sauce for serving (optional)

Instructions:

1. In a large pot, heat 2 tablespoons of olive oil over medium heat. Add the thinly sliced onions and cook, stirring occasionally, until they are caramelized and golden brown, about 20-25 minutes. Be patient, as caramelizing the onions slowly is key to developing their sweetness and depth of flavor. Once caramelized, transfer the onions to a plate and set aside.
2. In the same pot, heat the remaining 2 tablespoons of olive oil over medium heat. Add the rinsed lentils and rice, and toast them for a few minutes, stirring occasionally, until they are lightly golden.
3. Pour in the vegetable broth or water, and add the ground cumin, ground coriander, ground cinnamon, salt, and pepper. Stir to combine.
4. Bring the mixture to a boil, then reduce the heat to low. Cover the pot and let the Mujadara simmer for about 20-25 minutes, or until the lentils and rice are tender and the liquid has been absorbed.
5. Once cooked, remove the pot from the heat and let it sit, covered, for 5 minutes to allow the Mujadara to steam.
6. Fluff the Mujadara with a fork, then gently fold in half of the caramelized onions.
7. Transfer the Mujadara to a serving platter or individual plates. Garnish with the remaining caramelized onions and chopped fresh parsley or cilantro, if desired.

8. Serve the Mujadara hot, accompanied by yogurt or tahini sauce on the side if desired.

Enjoy the comforting and flavorful Mujadara as a main dish or as a side dish alongside grilled vegetables, salad, or your favorite Middle Eastern dishes.

Schnitzel with lemon sauce

Ingredients:

For the schnitzel:

- 4 boneless, skinless chicken breasts or pork chops, pounded to about 1/4 inch thickness
- 1 cup all-purpose flour
- 2 eggs, beaten
- 1 cup breadcrumbs (plain or seasoned)
- Salt and pepper to taste
- Vegetable oil for frying

For the lemon sauce:

- 1/4 cup unsalted butter
- 2 cloves garlic, minced
- 1/4 cup chicken broth
- Juice of 2 lemons
- Zest of 1 lemon
- 2 tablespoons chopped fresh parsley
- Salt and pepper to taste

Instructions:

1. Preheat your oven to 200°F (93°C) to keep the schnitzels warm while you prepare the lemon sauce.
2. Season the pounded chicken breasts or pork chops with salt and pepper on both sides.
3. Set up a breading station with three shallow bowls: one with flour, one with beaten eggs, and one with breadcrumbs.
4. Dredge each piece of chicken or pork in the flour, shaking off any excess, then dip it into the beaten eggs, and finally coat it evenly with breadcrumbs, pressing gently to adhere. Repeat with the remaining pieces.

5. Heat vegetable oil in a large skillet over medium-high heat. Once the oil is hot, add the breaded chicken or pork pieces in batches, being careful not to overcrowd the pan. Cook for 3-4 minutes on each side, or until golden brown and cooked through. Transfer the cooked schnitzels to a paper towel-lined plate to drain excess oil, then place them on a baking sheet and keep warm in the preheated oven.
6. In the same skillet, melt the unsalted butter over medium heat. Add the minced garlic and cook for about 1 minute, or until fragrant.
7. Stir in the chicken broth, lemon juice, lemon zest, chopped fresh parsley, salt, and pepper. Bring the sauce to a simmer and cook for an additional 2-3 minutes, stirring occasionally, until slightly thickened.
8. Taste the lemon sauce and adjust the seasoning if needed, adding more salt, pepper, or lemon juice according to your preference.
9. Remove the schnitzels from the oven and transfer them to serving plates.
10. Spoon the lemon sauce over the schnitzels just before serving.

Enjoy the crispy schnitzels with the tangy and aromatic lemon sauce, served with your favorite sides such as mashed potatoes, steamed vegetables, or a fresh salad.

Israeli chopped salad

Ingredients:

- 2 large tomatoes, diced
- 1 cucumber, diced
- 1 bell pepper (red, yellow, or green), diced
- 1 small red onion, finely diced
- 1/4 cup fresh parsley, chopped
- 1/4 cup fresh mint, chopped
- Juice of 1-2 lemons
- 2 tablespoons extra virgin olive oil
- Salt and black pepper to taste

Instructions:

1. In a large mixing bowl, combine the diced tomatoes, diced cucumber, diced bell pepper, finely diced red onion, chopped parsley, and chopped mint.
2. In a small bowl, whisk together the lemon juice and extra virgin olive oil to make the dressing. Season with salt and black pepper to taste.
3. Pour the dressing over the chopped vegetables in the mixing bowl.
4. Toss the salad until all the ingredients are well coated with the dressing.
5. Taste the salad and adjust the seasoning if needed, adding more salt, pepper, or lemon juice according to your preference.
6. Cover the bowl and refrigerate the Israeli chopped salad for at least 30 minutes to allow the flavors to meld.
7. Before serving, give the salad a final toss and transfer it to a serving bowl or platter.
8. Garnish the Israeli chopped salad with additional chopped herbs, if desired.
9. Serve the salad chilled as a refreshing side dish or light meal.

Enjoy the colorful and flavorful Israeli chopped salad as a fresh and healthy addition to any meal! It pairs well with grilled meats, falafel, hummus, pita bread, or as part of a mezze platter.

Bourekas (pastry filled with cheese or spinach)

Ingredients:

For the dough:

- 2 sheets of puff pastry dough, thawed if frozen
- Flour for dusting

For the cheese filling:

- 1 cup crumbled feta cheese
- 1 cup shredded mozzarella cheese
- 1/4 cup grated Parmesan cheese
- 1 egg, beaten (for egg wash)

For the spinach filling:

- 2 cups fresh spinach leaves, chopped
- 1 cup crumbled feta cheese
- 1/4 cup grated Parmesan cheese
- 1 egg, beaten (for egg wash)

For both fillings:

- 1 egg, beaten (for egg wash)
- Sesame seeds or poppy seeds for sprinkling (optional)

Instructions:

1. Preheat your oven to 375°F (190°C) and line a baking sheet with parchment paper.

2. If using frozen puff pastry dough, let it thaw according to the package instructions. Once thawed, lightly dust a clean work surface with flour and roll out the puff pastry sheets into rectangles, about 1/4 inch thick.
3. To make the cheese filling: In a mixing bowl, combine the crumbled feta cheese, shredded mozzarella cheese, and grated Parmesan cheese. Mix well to combine.
4. To make the spinach filling: In a separate mixing bowl, combine the chopped spinach leaves, crumbled feta cheese, and grated Parmesan cheese. Mix well to combine.
5. Cut each rolled-out puff pastry sheet into squares or rectangles, depending on your preference and the size of the pastries you want to make.
6. Spoon a small amount of the desired filling (cheese or spinach) onto one half of each puff pastry square or rectangle, leaving a border around the edges.
7. Fold the other half of the puff pastry over the filling to form a triangle or rectangle shape, depending on the shape of your pastry.
8. Press the edges of the pastry together firmly to seal, then use a fork to crimp the edges for a decorative finish.
9. Place the filled pastries on the prepared baking sheet, leaving some space between them.
10. Brush the tops of the pastries with beaten egg, then sprinkle with sesame seeds or poppy seeds if desired.
11. Bake the bourekas in the preheated oven for 20-25 minutes, or until they are golden brown and puffed up.
12. Once baked, remove the bourekas from the oven and let them cool slightly on the baking sheet before serving.

Enjoy the delicious and flaky bourekas filled with cheese or spinach as a snack, appetizer, or part of a brunch spread! They are best served warm or at room temperature.

Stuffed peppers with rice and beef

Ingredients:

- 4 large bell peppers (any color), tops removed and seeds removed
- 1 lb ground beef (or ground turkey)
- 1 cup cooked rice (white or brown)
- 1 onion, finely chopped
- 2 cloves garlic, minced
- 1 can (14.5 oz) diced tomatoes, drained
- 1 cup tomato sauce
- 1 teaspoon dried oregano
- 1 teaspoon dried basil
- 1/2 teaspoon paprika
- Salt and pepper to taste
- 1 cup shredded cheese (cheddar, mozzarella, or a blend)
- Fresh parsley or basil for garnish (optional)

Instructions:

1. Preheat your oven to 375°F (190°C). Lightly grease a baking dish large enough to hold the stuffed peppers.
2. In a large skillet, cook the ground beef over medium heat until browned. Drain any excess fat.
3. Add the chopped onion and minced garlic to the skillet with the cooked ground beef. Cook for 2-3 minutes, or until the onion is softened and translucent.
4. Stir in the cooked rice, diced tomatoes, tomato sauce, dried oregano, dried basil, paprika, salt, and pepper. Cook for an additional 5 minutes, stirring occasionally, to allow the flavors to meld.
5. Remove the skillet from the heat and let the filling mixture cool slightly.
6. Stuff each bell pepper with the beef and rice mixture, pressing down gently to fill the peppers evenly. Place the stuffed peppers upright in the prepared baking dish.
7. If desired, sprinkle shredded cheese over the tops of the stuffed peppers.
8. Cover the baking dish with aluminum foil and bake in the preheated oven for 30-35 minutes, or until the peppers are tender and the filling is heated through.

9. Remove the foil and continue baking for an additional 5-10 minutes, or until the cheese is melted and bubbly.
10. Once cooked, remove the stuffed peppers from the oven and let them cool slightly before serving.
11. Garnish the stuffed peppers with fresh parsley or basil, if desired, before serving.

Enjoy the delicious and comforting stuffed peppers with rice and beef as a satisfying main dish! They are versatile and can be customized with your favorite ingredients and seasonings.

Moroccan fish tagine

Ingredients:

- 1 lb firm white fish fillets (such as cod, haddock, or tilapia), cut into large chunks
- 2 tablespoons olive oil
- 1 onion, finely chopped
- 2 cloves garlic, minced
- 1 teaspoon ground cumin
- 1 teaspoon ground coriander
- 1 teaspoon ground paprika
- 1/2 teaspoon ground turmeric
- 1/2 teaspoon ground cinnamon
- 1/4 teaspoon ground ginger
- Pinch of saffron threads (optional)
- 1 can (14 oz) diced tomatoes, with their juices
- 1 cup fish or vegetable broth
- 1/4 cup green olives, pitted
- 1/4 cup raisins or chopped dried apricots (optional)
- Zest and juice of 1 lemon
- Salt and pepper to taste
- Fresh cilantro or parsley, chopped, for garnish
- Cooked couscous or crusty bread, for serving

Instructions:

1. Heat the olive oil in a large tagine or heavy-bottomed pot over medium heat. Add the chopped onion and cook until softened, about 5 minutes.
2. Add the minced garlic, ground cumin, ground coriander, ground paprika, ground turmeric, ground cinnamon, ground ginger, and saffron threads (if using). Cook for another 2 minutes, stirring frequently, until fragrant.
3. Stir in the diced tomatoes with their juices and the fish or vegetable broth. Bring the mixture to a simmer.
4. Gently add the fish chunks to the tagine or pot, nestling them into the sauce. Season with salt and pepper.
5. Scatter the green olives and raisins or chopped dried apricots (if using) over the top of the fish.

6. Cover the tagine or pot and let the fish simmer gently for 10-15 minutes, or until the fish is cooked through and flakes easily with a fork.
7. Just before serving, stir in the lemon zest and lemon juice to brighten the flavors.
8. Garnish the Moroccan fish tagine with chopped fresh cilantro or parsley.
9. Serve the fish tagine hot, with cooked couscous or crusty bread on the side to soak up the flavorful sauce.

Enjoy the rich and aromatic flavors of Moroccan fish tagine as a comforting and satisfying meal! It's perfect for a cozy dinner with family and friends.

Israeli-style stuffed chicken breast

Ingredients:

- 4 boneless, skinless chicken breasts
- Salt and pepper to taste
- 1 tablespoon olive oil

For the filling:

- 1 cup cooked quinoa or rice
- 1/2 cup crumbled feta cheese
- 1/4 cup chopped sun-dried tomatoes
- 1/4 cup chopped Kalamata olives
- 2 tablespoons chopped fresh parsley
- 1 teaspoon dried oregano
- 1 teaspoon garlic powder
- Salt and pepper to taste

Instructions:

1. Preheat your oven to 375°F (190°C). Lightly grease a baking dish large enough to hold the stuffed chicken breasts.
2. In a mixing bowl, combine the cooked quinoa or rice, crumbled feta cheese, chopped sun-dried tomatoes, chopped Kalamata olives, chopped fresh parsley, dried oregano, garlic powder, salt, and pepper. Mix well to combine.
3. Using a sharp knife, make a horizontal slit along the side of each chicken breast to create a pocket for the filling. Be careful not to cut all the way through.
4. Season the inside of each chicken breast with salt and pepper.
5. Stuff each chicken breast with the filling mixture, dividing it evenly among the breasts. Press the edges of the chicken together to seal in the filling.
6. Heat the olive oil in a large skillet over medium-high heat. Once hot, add the stuffed chicken breasts to the skillet and cook for 2-3 minutes on each side, or until they are lightly browned.
7. Transfer the browned chicken breasts to the prepared baking dish.

8. Bake the stuffed chicken breasts in the preheated oven for 20-25 minutes, or until they are cooked through and the internal temperature reaches 165°F (74°C).
9. Once cooked, remove the stuffed chicken breasts from the oven and let them rest for a few minutes before serving.
10. Serve the Israeli-style stuffed chicken breasts hot, garnished with additional chopped parsley if desired.

Enjoy the delicious and flavorful Israeli-style stuffed chicken breasts as a satisfying main dish! They pair well with a variety of sides such as roasted vegetables, couscous, or a fresh salad.

Spinach and cheese burekas

Ingredients:

For the dough:

- 2 sheets of puff pastry dough, thawed if frozen
- Flour for dusting

For the filling:

- 1 tablespoon olive oil
- 1 small onion, finely chopped
- 2 cloves garlic, minced
- 4 cups fresh spinach leaves, chopped
- 1 cup crumbled feta cheese
- 1 cup shredded mozzarella cheese
- Salt and pepper to taste

For assembling:

- 1 egg, beaten (for egg wash)
- Sesame seeds or poppy seeds for sprinkling (optional)

Instructions:

1. Preheat your oven to 375°F (190°C). Line a baking sheet with parchment paper.
2. Heat the olive oil in a skillet over medium heat. Add the chopped onion and minced garlic, and sauté until softened, about 2-3 minutes.
3. Add the chopped spinach leaves to the skillet and cook until wilted, about 2-3 minutes. Remove from heat and let cool slightly.
4. In a mixing bowl, combine the cooked spinach mixture, crumbled feta cheese, shredded mozzarella cheese, salt, and pepper. Mix well to combine.
5. Lightly dust a clean work surface with flour. Roll out the puff pastry sheets into rectangles, about 1/4 inch thick.
6. Cut each rolled-out puff pastry sheet into squares or rectangles, depending on your preference and the size of the burekas you want to make.

7. Place a spoonful of the spinach and cheese filling onto one half of each puff pastry square or rectangle, leaving a border around the edges.
8. Fold the other half of the puff pastry over the filling to form a triangle or rectangle shape, depending on the shape of your pastry.
9. Press the edges of the pastry together firmly to seal, then use a fork to crimp the edges for a decorative finish.
10. Place the assembled burekas on the prepared baking sheet.
11. Brush the tops of the burekas with beaten egg, then sprinkle with sesame seeds or poppy seeds if desired.
12. Bake the burekas in the preheated oven for 20-25 minutes, or until they are golden brown and puffed up.
13. Once baked, remove the burekas from the oven and let them cool slightly on the baking sheet before serving.

Enjoy the delicious and savory spinach and cheese burekas as a snack, appetizer, or part of a brunch spread! They are best served warm or at room temperature.

Kebab in pita with tahini sauce

Ingredients:

For the kebab:

- 1 lb ground lamb or beef
- 1 small onion, grated
- 2 cloves garlic, minced
- 1 teaspoon ground cumin
- 1 teaspoon ground coriander
- 1/2 teaspoon paprika
- 1/2 teaspoon ground cinnamon
- Salt and pepper to taste
- Olive oil for cooking

For the tahini sauce:

- 1/2 cup tahini paste
- 1/4 cup water
- 2 tablespoons lemon juice
- 1 clove garlic, minced
- Salt to taste

For serving:

- Pita bread
- Sliced tomatoes
- Sliced cucumbers
- Chopped lettuce
- Chopped parsley or cilantro
- Pickles (optional)
- Hot sauce or chili flakes (optional)

Instructions:

1. In a mixing bowl, combine the ground lamb or beef, grated onion, minced garlic, ground cumin, ground coriander, paprika, ground cinnamon, salt, and pepper. Mix well to combine.
2. Shape the meat mixture into small elongated kebabs or patties.
3. Heat a grill pan or skillet over medium-high heat. Brush the pan with olive oil.
4. Cook the kebabs for 4-5 minutes on each side, or until they are cooked through and have a nice charred exterior. Alternatively, you can grill the kebabs on an outdoor grill.
5. While the kebabs are cooking, prepare the tahini sauce. In a small bowl, whisk together the tahini paste, water, lemon juice, minced garlic, and salt until smooth and creamy. Add more water if needed to reach your desired consistency.
6. Warm the pita bread in a toaster or oven until soft and pliable.
7. To assemble the kebab in pita sandwiches, spread a generous amount of tahini sauce inside each pita bread.
8. Place a few slices of tomato, cucumber, and chopped lettuce inside each pita.
9. Place one or two cooked kebabs on top of the vegetables.
10. Garnish with chopped parsley or cilantro, and add pickles and hot sauce or chili flakes if desired.
11. Serve the kebab in pita sandwiches immediately, while warm.

Enjoy the delicious and satisfying kebab in pita with tahini sauce as a flavorful meal or snack!

Potato latkes

Ingredients:

- 4 large russet potatoes, peeled
- 1 onion, peeled
- 2 eggs, beaten
- 1/4 cup all-purpose flour or matzo meal
- 1 teaspoon salt, or to taste
- 1/2 teaspoon black pepper, or to taste
- Vegetable oil for frying

Instructions:

1. Grate the peeled potatoes and onion using a box grater or a food processor fitted with a grating attachment. Transfer the grated potatoes and onion to a clean kitchen towel or cheesecloth and squeeze out as much moisture as possible.
2. In a large mixing bowl, combine the grated and drained potatoes and onion with the beaten eggs, flour or matzo meal, salt, and black pepper. Mix well to combine.
3. Heat about 1/4 inch of vegetable oil in a large skillet over medium-high heat until hot but not smoking.
4. Take about 1/4 cup of the potato mixture and form it into a pancake shape. Carefully place the pancake into the hot oil and flatten it slightly with a spatula.
5. Repeat with the remaining potato mixture, making sure not to overcrowd the skillet. You may need to fry the latkes in batches, adding more oil to the skillet as needed.
6. Fry the latkes for 3-4 minutes on each side, or until they are golden brown and crispy.
7. Once cooked, transfer the latkes to a paper towel-lined plate to drain any excess oil.
8. Serve the potato latkes hot, with applesauce, sour cream, or your favorite topping on the side.

Enjoy the crispy and delicious potato latkes as a snack, appetizer, or side dish! They are best served fresh and hot.

Grilled halloumi cheese with honey

Ingredients:

1 block of halloumi cheese, sliced into thick slices

2 tablespoons olive oil

2 tablespoons honey

Fresh herbs for garnish (optional)

Lemon wedges for serving (optional)

Instructions:

Preheat your grill or grill pan to medium-high heat.

Brush the slices of halloumi cheese with olive oil on both sides to prevent sticking.

Place the halloumi cheese slices directly onto the grill or grill pan. Cook for 2-3 minutes on each side, or until grill marks form and the cheese is heated through.

While the halloumi cheese is grilling, warm the honey in a small saucepan or microwave until it is thin and pourable.

Once the halloumi cheese is grilled to your liking, transfer it to a serving platter.

Drizzle the warm honey over the grilled halloumi cheese slices.

Garnish with fresh herbs, such as chopped parsley or thyme, if desired.

Serve the grilled halloumi cheese with honey immediately, with lemon wedges on the side for squeezing over the cheese if desired.

Enjoy the delicious combination of salty halloumi cheese and sweet honey as a tasty appetizer or snack! It's perfect for summer grilling or any time you're craving a simple and satisfying dish.

Israeli vegetable tagine

Ingredients:

- 2 tablespoons olive oil
- 1 onion, finely chopped
- 2 cloves garlic, minced
- 1 teaspoon ground cumin
- 1 teaspoon ground coriander
- 1/2 teaspoon ground turmeric
- 1/2 teaspoon ground cinnamon
- 1/4 teaspoon ground ginger
- Pinch of saffron threads (optional)
- 2 carrots, peeled and sliced
- 2 potatoes, peeled and diced
- 1 sweet potato, peeled and diced
- 1 zucchini, diced
- 1 yellow squash, diced
- 1 bell pepper (red, yellow, or green), diced
- 1 can (14 oz) diced tomatoes, with their juices
- 2 cups vegetable broth
- 1 cup cooked chickpeas (optional)
- Salt and pepper to taste
- Chopped fresh cilantro or parsley for garnish

Instructions:

1. Heat the olive oil in a large tagine or heavy-bottomed pot over medium heat.
2. Add the chopped onion to the tagine or pot and sauté until softened, about 5 minutes.
3. Add the minced garlic, ground cumin, ground coriander, ground turmeric, ground cinnamon, ground ginger, and saffron threads (if using). Cook for another 2 minutes, stirring frequently, until fragrant.
4. Add the sliced carrots, diced potatoes, diced sweet potato, diced zucchini, diced yellow squash, and diced bell pepper to the tagine or pot. Stir to coat the vegetables with the spices.

5. Pour in the diced tomatoes with their juices and vegetable broth. Stir in the cooked chickpeas if using. Season with salt and pepper to taste.
6. Cover the tagine or pot and let the vegetable mixture simmer gently for about 20-25 minutes, or until the vegetables are tender.
7. Once the vegetables are cooked, remove the tagine or pot from the heat.
8. Garnish the Israeli vegetable tagine with chopped fresh cilantro or parsley before serving.
9. Serve the vegetable tagine hot, accompanied by couscous, rice, or crusty bread.

Enjoy the flavorful and comforting Israeli vegetable tagine as a satisfying vegetarian main dish or as a side dish alongside grilled meats or fish.

Lemon herb roasted chicken

Ingredients:

- 1 whole chicken (about 4-5 lbs)
- 2 lemons, quartered
- 4 cloves garlic, minced
- 2 tablespoons fresh rosemary, chopped
- 2 tablespoons fresh thyme leaves
- 2 tablespoons fresh parsley, chopped
- 2 tablespoons olive oil
- Salt and pepper to taste

Instructions:

1. Preheat your oven to 425°F (220°C). Place a rack in a roasting pan and lightly grease the rack with cooking spray or oil.
2. Rinse the chicken inside and out under cold running water and pat it dry with paper towels. Place the chicken on the prepared rack in the roasting pan.
3. In a small bowl, combine the minced garlic, chopped rosemary, thyme leaves, chopped parsley, olive oil, salt, and pepper to create the herb mixture.
4. Rub the herb mixture all over the surface of the chicken, including the cavity. Be sure to coat the chicken evenly with the mixture.
5. Stuff the cavity of the chicken with the quartered lemons.
6. Tie the legs of the chicken together with kitchen twine, if desired, to help the chicken cook evenly.
7. Place the roasting pan in the preheated oven and roast the chicken for about 1 hour to 1 hour and 15 minutes, or until the internal temperature reaches 165°F (74°C) in the thickest part of the thigh and the juices run clear when pierced with a knife.
8. If the skin starts to brown too quickly during cooking, cover the chicken loosely with aluminum foil.
9. Once cooked, remove the roasting pan from the oven and let the chicken rest for about 10 minutes before carving.
10. Carve the lemon herb roasted chicken and serve it with your favorite sides, such as roasted vegetables, mashed potatoes, or a fresh salad.

Enjoy the tender and flavorful lemon herb roasted chicken as a comforting and satisfying meal! The combination of lemon and fresh herbs adds brightness and depth of flavor to the dish.

Israeli-style meatballs in tomato sauce

Ingredients:

For the meatballs:

- 1 lb ground beef or lamb
- 1 small onion, finely chopped
- 2 cloves garlic, minced
- 1/4 cup breadcrumbs
- 1/4 cup chopped fresh parsley
- 1 egg, lightly beaten
- 1 teaspoon ground cumin
- 1 teaspoon ground coriander
- 1/2 teaspoon paprika
- Salt and pepper to taste
- Olive oil for frying

For the tomato sauce:

- 2 tablespoons olive oil
- 1 onion, finely chopped
- 2 cloves garlic, minced
- 1 can (14 oz) crushed tomatoes
- 1 can (6 oz) tomato paste
- 1 teaspoon dried oregano
- 1 teaspoon dried basil
- 1/2 teaspoon paprika
- Salt and pepper to taste
- 1 cup beef or vegetable broth
- Chopped fresh parsley for garnish (optional)

Instructions:

1. In a large mixing bowl, combine the ground beef or lamb, finely chopped onion, minced garlic, breadcrumbs, chopped parsley, beaten egg, ground cumin, ground coriander, paprika, salt, and pepper. Mix until well combined.
2. Shape the meat mixture into small meatballs, about 1 inch in diameter.
3. Heat a drizzle of olive oil in a large skillet over medium-high heat. Once hot, add the meatballs in batches and cook until browned on all sides, about 4-5 minutes per batch. Transfer the browned meatballs to a plate and set aside.
4. In the same skillet, add another drizzle of olive oil if needed. Add the finely chopped onion and minced garlic, and sauté until softened, about 2-3 minutes.
5. Stir in the crushed tomatoes, tomato paste, dried oregano, dried basil, paprika, salt, and pepper. Cook for another 2 minutes, stirring occasionally.
6. Pour in the beef or vegetable broth and stir to combine. Bring the sauce to a simmer.
7. Return the browned meatballs to the skillet, nestling them into the sauce.
8. Cover the skillet and let the meatballs simmer in the sauce for about 15-20 minutes, or until cooked through and the sauce has thickened slightly.
9. Once cooked, remove the skillet from the heat.
10. Serve the Israeli-style meatballs in tomato sauce hot, garnished with chopped fresh parsley if desired.

Enjoy the delicious and comforting Israeli-style meatballs in tomato sauce as a hearty main dish! They pair well with pasta, couscous, or crusty bread for soaking up the flavorful sauce.

Grilled lamb chops with mint sauce

Ingredients:

For the lamb chops:

- 8 lamb loin chops, about 1 inch thick
- 2 tablespoons olive oil
- 2 cloves garlic, minced
- 1 teaspoon dried rosemary
- 1 teaspoon dried thyme
- Salt and pepper to taste

For the mint sauce:

- 1/2 cup fresh mint leaves, chopped
- 2 tablespoons fresh parsley, chopped
- 2 tablespoons red wine vinegar
- 1 tablespoon honey
- 1 tablespoon Dijon mustard
- 1 clove garlic, minced
- 1/4 cup olive oil
- Salt and pepper to taste

Instructions:

1. Preheat your grill to medium-high heat.
2. In a small bowl, combine the olive oil, minced garlic, dried rosemary, dried thyme, salt, and pepper. Mix well to make a marinade.
3. Pat the lamb chops dry with paper towels and place them in a shallow dish. Pour the marinade over the lamb chops, turning to coat evenly. Let the lamb chops marinate for at least 30 minutes at room temperature, or refrigerate for up to 4 hours.
4. While the lamb chops are marinating, prepare the mint sauce. In a blender or food processor, combine the chopped mint leaves, chopped parsley, red wine vinegar, honey, Dijon mustard, minced garlic, olive oil, salt, and pepper. Blend until

smooth. Taste and adjust seasoning if needed. Transfer the mint sauce to a serving bowl and set aside.
5. Remove the lamb chops from the marinade and discard any excess marinade.
6. Place the lamb chops on the preheated grill and cook for 3-4 minutes per side for medium-rare, or until they reach your desired level of doneness.
7. Once cooked, transfer the grilled lamb chops to a serving platter and let them rest for a few minutes.
8. Serve the grilled lamb chops hot, accompanied by the mint sauce on the side for dipping or drizzling.

Enjoy the juicy and flavorful grilled lamb chops with mint sauce as a delicious main course! Serve them with your favorite sides, such as roasted vegetables, couscous, or a fresh salad, for a complete meal.

Falafel burger

Ingredients:

For the falafel patties:

- 2 cans (15 oz each) chickpeas, drained and rinsed
- 1 small onion, chopped
- 3 cloves garlic, minced
- 1/4 cup chopped fresh parsley
- 1/4 cup chopped fresh cilantro
- 1 teaspoon ground cumin
- 1 teaspoon ground coriander
- 1/2 teaspoon baking powder
- 1/4 teaspoon cayenne pepper (optional)
- Salt and pepper to taste
- 2-3 tablespoons all-purpose flour or chickpea flour, if needed
- Olive oil for frying

For assembling the burger:

- Burger buns
- Lettuce leaves
- Sliced tomatoes
- Sliced cucumbers
- Sliced red onion
- Tzatziki sauce or tahini sauce
- Additional toppings of your choice (pickles, avocado, etc.)

Instructions:

1. In a food processor, combine the drained and rinsed chickpeas, chopped onion, minced garlic, chopped parsley, chopped cilantro, ground cumin, ground coriander, baking powder, cayenne pepper (if using), salt, and pepper. Pulse until the mixture is well combined but still slightly chunky.

2. Transfer the falafel mixture to a bowl. If the mixture is too wet to form into patties, add 2-3 tablespoons of all-purpose flour or chickpea flour and mix until the mixture holds together.
3. Divide the falafel mixture into equal portions and shape each portion into a patty, about 1/2 inch thick.
4. Heat a thin layer of olive oil in a large skillet over medium heat. Once hot, add the falafel patties to the skillet in batches, making sure not to overcrowd the pan. Cook the patties for 3-4 minutes on each side, or until they are golden brown and crispy. Transfer the cooked patties to a plate lined with paper towels to drain any excess oil.
5. Assemble the falafel burgers by placing a lettuce leaf on the bottom half of each burger bun. Top with a falafel patty, sliced tomatoes, sliced cucumbers, sliced red onion, and a dollop of tzatziki sauce or tahini sauce. Add any additional toppings of your choice.
6. Place the top half of the burger bun on top of the toppings to complete the burger.
7. Serve the falafel burgers immediately, with extra sauce on the side for dipping, if desired.

Enjoy the flavorful and satisfying falafel burgers as a delicious vegetarian meal option!

They're perfect for lunch, dinner, or anytime you're craving a tasty burger with a twist.

Chicken schnitzel sandwich

Ingredients:

For the chicken schnitzel:

- 2 boneless, skinless chicken breasts
- Salt and pepper to taste
- 1/2 cup all-purpose flour
- 2 eggs, beaten
- 1 cup breadcrumbs (plain or seasoned)
- Vegetable oil for frying

For assembling the sandwich:

- Sandwich buns or bread of your choice
- Lettuce leaves
- Sliced tomatoes
- Sliced red onion
- Pickles
- Mayonnaise
- Mustard
- Optional: Cheese slices (such as Swiss or cheddar)

Instructions:

1. Place each chicken breast between two sheets of plastic wrap or parchment paper. Use a meat mallet or rolling pin to pound the chicken breasts until they are about 1/4 inch thick. This helps to ensure even cooking and tenderness.
2. Season both sides of the chicken breasts with salt and pepper.
3. Set up a breading station with three shallow dishes: one containing the all-purpose flour, one containing the beaten eggs, and one containing the breadcrumbs.
4. Dredge each chicken breast in the flour, shaking off any excess. Dip it into the beaten eggs, allowing any excess to drip off. Finally, coat the chicken breast evenly in the breadcrumbs, pressing gently to adhere.

5. Heat vegetable oil in a large skillet over medium-high heat. Once hot, add the breaded chicken breasts to the skillet. Cook for 3-4 minutes on each side, or until golden brown and cooked through. The internal temperature of the chicken should reach 165°F (74°C).
6. Once cooked, transfer the chicken schnitzel to a plate lined with paper towels to drain any excess oil.
7. To assemble the sandwich, spread mayonnaise and mustard on the bottom half of each sandwich bun or bread slice.
8. Place a piece of lettuce on top of the sauce, followed by a chicken schnitzel. Top with sliced tomatoes, sliced red onion, pickles, and cheese slices if using.
9. Close the sandwich with the top half of the bun or bread slice.
10. Serve the chicken schnitzel sandwiches immediately, with additional condiments or toppings as desired.

Enjoy the crispy and flavorful chicken schnitzel sandwich as a satisfying meal for lunch or dinner! It's perfect for picnics, gatherings, or anytime you're craving a delicious sandwich.

Shakshuka with feta cheese

Ingredients:

- 2 tablespoons olive oil
- 1 onion, diced
- 2 cloves garlic, minced
- 1 bell pepper, diced (red, yellow, or green)
- 1 teaspoon ground cumin
- 1 teaspoon paprika
- 1/2 teaspoon ground coriander
- 1/4 teaspoon cayenne pepper (optional, for extra heat)
- 1 can (14 oz) diced tomatoes
- 1 tablespoon tomato paste
- Salt and pepper to taste
- 4-6 large eggs
- 1/2 cup crumbled feta cheese
- Chopped fresh parsley or cilantro for garnish
- Crusty bread or pita for serving

Instructions:

1. Heat the olive oil in a large skillet or cast-iron pan over medium heat.
2. Add the diced onion to the skillet and sauté until translucent, about 5 minutes.
3. Add the minced garlic and diced bell pepper to the skillet, and cook for another 2-3 minutes until the vegetables are softened.
4. Stir in the ground cumin, paprika, ground coriander, and cayenne pepper (if using). Cook for 1 minute until fragrant.
5. Add the diced tomatoes and tomato paste to the skillet, and stir to combine. Season with salt and pepper to taste.
6. Simmer the tomato mixture for 10-15 minutes, stirring occasionally, until the sauce has thickened slightly.
7. Use a spoon to create small wells or indentations in the tomato sauce. Crack one egg into each indentation.
8. Cover the skillet and cook for 5-7 minutes, or until the egg whites are set but the yolks are still runny. Cooking time may vary depending on how runny you like your eggs.

9. Sprinkle the crumbled feta cheese evenly over the top of the shakshuka.
10. Garnish the shakshuka with chopped fresh parsley or cilantro.
11. Serve the shakshuka hot, directly from the skillet, with crusty bread or pita for dipping.

Enjoy the flavorful and comforting Shakshuka with feta cheese as a satisfying breakfast, brunch, or dinner option! It's perfect for sharing with family and friends.

Sabich bowl (deconstructed sabich)

Ingredients:

For the roasted eggplant:

- 1 large eggplant, sliced into rounds
- Olive oil
- Salt and pepper to taste
- 1 teaspoon ground cumin
- 1/2 teaspoon paprika

For the bowl:

- Cooked quinoa or rice
- Hard-boiled eggs, sliced
- Hummus
- Israeli salad (diced tomatoes, cucumbers, onions, parsley)
- Pickled cucumbers or pickled onions
- Tahini sauce
- Fresh parsley or cilantro for garnish
- Optional: Pita bread or pita chips for serving

Instructions:

1. Preheat your oven to 400°F (200°C). Line a baking sheet with parchment paper.
2. Place the sliced eggplant rounds on the prepared baking sheet. Drizzle with olive oil and season with salt, pepper, ground cumin, and paprika.
3. Roast the eggplant in the preheated oven for 20-25 minutes, or until tender and golden brown.
4. While the eggplant is roasting, prepare the other components of the Sabich bowl.
5. Cook the quinoa or rice according to package instructions.
6. Make the Israeli salad by combining diced tomatoes, cucumbers, onions, and parsley in a bowl. Season with salt and pepper to taste.
7. Slice the hard-boiled eggs.

8. Assemble the Sabich bowl by dividing the cooked quinoa or rice among serving bowls.
9. Top each bowl with roasted eggplant slices, sliced hard-boiled eggs, Israeli salad, pickled cucumbers or onions, and a dollop of hummus and tahini sauce.
10. Garnish the bowls with fresh parsley or cilantro.
11. Serve the Sabich bowls with pita bread or pita chips on the side, if desired.

Enjoy the delicious and nutritious Sabich bowls as a satisfying meal for lunch or dinner! They're packed with flavor and textures, and you can customize them with your favorite toppings and additions.

Jerusalem mixed grill

Ingredients:

- 1 lb boneless, skinless chicken breasts
- 1 lb lamb shoulder or leg meat, cut into cubes
- 1 lb beef sirloin or ribeye steak, cut into cubes
- 1 onion, sliced
- 1 bell pepper (red, yellow, or green), sliced
- 1 zucchini, sliced
- 1 eggplant, sliced
- Olive oil
- Salt and pepper to taste
- Lemon wedges for serving
- Optional: Pita bread or flatbread for serving

Marinade:

- 1/4 cup olive oil
- 2 cloves garlic, minced
- 1 teaspoon ground cumin
- 1 teaspoon ground coriander
- 1 teaspoon paprika
- 1/2 teaspoon ground turmeric
- 1/2 teaspoon ground cinnamon
- Salt and pepper to taste
- Juice of 1 lemon

Instructions:

1. In a large bowl, combine the olive oil, minced garlic, ground cumin, ground coriander, paprika, ground turmeric, ground cinnamon, salt, pepper, and lemon juice to make the marinade.
2. Place the chicken, lamb, and beef cubes in separate bowls. Pour a portion of the marinade over each type of meat, ensuring they are well coated. Cover the bowls

and let the meats marinate in the refrigerator for at least 1 hour, or preferably overnight.
3. Preheat your grill to medium-high heat. If using wooden skewers, soak them in water for at least 30 minutes to prevent burning.
4. Thread the marinated meat cubes onto skewers, alternating with slices of onion, bell pepper, zucchini, and eggplant.
5. Brush the vegetables with olive oil and season with salt and pepper.
6. Place the skewers on the preheated grill and cook for 8-10 minutes, turning occasionally, or until the meats are cooked to your desired doneness and the vegetables are tender and slightly charred.
7. Once cooked, remove the skewers from the grill and let them rest for a few minutes.
8. Serve the Jerusalem mixed grill hot, with lemon wedges on the side for squeezing over the meat and vegetables.
9. Optionally, serve the mixed grill with warm pita bread or flatbread to soak up the juices and enjoy as a sandwich.

Enjoy the flavorful and aromatic Jerusalem mixed grill as a satisfying main dish for a barbecue or any occasion! It's a delicious way to enjoy a variety of grilled meats and vegetables with Middle Eastern flavors.

Tabbouleh salad

Ingredients:

- 1 cup bulgur wheat
- 2 cups boiling water
- 1/4 cup lemon juice (about 2 lemons)
- 1/4 cup extra virgin olive oil
- 2 cloves garlic, minced
- Salt and pepper to taste
- 1 large bunch flat-leaf parsley, finely chopped (about 2 cups chopped)
- 1/2 cup fresh mint leaves, finely chopped
- 2 large tomatoes, diced
- 1/2 English cucumber, diced
- 1/2 red onion, finely chopped
- Optional: 1/4 cup chopped green onions or scallions
- Optional: 1/4 cup chopped fresh dill
- Optional: 1/4 cup chopped fresh cilantro

Instructions:

1. Place the bulgur wheat in a large heatproof bowl. Pour the boiling water over the bulgur wheat, cover, and let it sit for about 20-30 minutes, or until the bulgur is tender and has absorbed all the water. Fluff the bulgur with a fork and let it cool to room temperature.
2. In a small bowl, whisk together the lemon juice, olive oil, minced garlic, salt, and pepper to make the dressing. Adjust the seasoning to taste.
3. In a large mixing bowl, combine the cooled bulgur wheat, chopped parsley, chopped mint, diced tomatoes, diced cucumber, chopped red onion, and any optional herbs you are using.
4. Pour the dressing over the salad ingredients and toss everything together until well combined and evenly coated with the dressing.
5. Taste the tabbouleh salad and adjust the seasoning if needed, adding more salt, pepper, or lemon juice as desired.
6. Cover the tabbouleh salad and refrigerate for at least 1 hour before serving to allow the flavors to meld together.

7. Before serving, give the tabbouleh salad a good toss and adjust the seasoning if needed. If the salad seems dry, you can drizzle a little more olive oil and lemon juice over the top.
8. Serve the tabbouleh salad chilled or at room temperature as a refreshing side dish or light meal.

Enjoy the fresh and vibrant flavors of homemade tabbouleh salad! It's perfect for picnics, potlucks, barbecues, or any occasion.

Shawarma bowl with rice and tahini sauce

Ingredients:

For the Shawarma chicken:

- 1 lb boneless, skinless chicken thighs, thinly sliced
- 2 tablespoons olive oil
- 2 cloves garlic, minced
- 1 teaspoon ground cumin
- 1 teaspoon ground coriander
- 1 teaspoon smoked paprika
- 1/2 teaspoon ground turmeric
- 1/2 teaspoon ground cinnamon
- Salt and pepper to taste
- Juice of 1 lemon

For the rice:

- 1 cup basmati rice
- 2 cups water or chicken broth
- Salt to taste

For the tahini sauce:

- 1/4 cup tahini paste
- 2 tablespoons lemon juice
- 1 clove garlic, minced
- 2-4 tablespoons water, as needed
- Salt to taste

For assembling the bowl:

- Cooked Shawarma chicken

- Cooked basmati rice
- Sliced cucumber
- Sliced tomatoes
- Sliced red onion
- Chopped fresh parsley or cilantro
- Optional: Pickled turnips, pickles, olives, hummus, pita bread

Instructions:

1. Marinate the Shawarma chicken: In a bowl, combine the olive oil, minced garlic, ground cumin, ground coriander, smoked paprika, ground turmeric, ground cinnamon, salt, pepper, and lemon juice. Add the thinly sliced chicken thighs and toss to coat. Cover and marinate in the refrigerator for at least 30 minutes, or up to overnight.
2. Prepare the rice: Rinse the basmati rice under cold water until the water runs clear. In a saucepan, combine the rinsed rice, water or chicken broth, and salt. Bring to a boil, then reduce the heat to low, cover, and simmer for 15-20 minutes, or until the rice is cooked and the liquid is absorbed. Fluff the rice with a fork and let it sit, covered, for 5 minutes before serving.
3. Make the tahini sauce: In a small bowl, whisk together the tahini paste, lemon juice, minced garlic, and salt. Gradually add water, 1 tablespoon at a time, until the sauce reaches your desired consistency. Taste and adjust the seasoning if needed.
4. Cook the Shawarma chicken: Heat a large skillet or grill pan over medium-high heat. Add the marinated chicken thighs and cook for 5-7 minutes, stirring occasionally, or until the chicken is cooked through and lightly browned.
5. Assemble the Shawarma bowl: Divide the cooked basmati rice among serving bowls. Top each bowl with the cooked Shawarma chicken, sliced cucumber, sliced tomatoes, sliced red onion, and any other desired toppings such as pickled turnips, pickles, or olives. Drizzle with tahini sauce and sprinkle with chopped fresh parsley or cilantro.
6. Serve: Serve the Shawarma bowls immediately, with optional sides like hummus and warm pita bread.

Enjoy the delicious and flavorful Shawarma bowl with rice and tahini sauce! It's a complete meal that's packed with Middle Eastern-inspired ingredients and perfect for lunch or dinner.

Stuffed eggplant with lamb and pine nuts

Ingredients:

- 2 large eggplants
- 1 lb ground lamb
- 1 onion, finely chopped
- 3 cloves garlic, minced
- 1/4 cup pine nuts
- 1 teaspoon ground cumin
- 1 teaspoon ground coriander
- 1/2 teaspoon ground cinnamon
- 1/4 teaspoon cayenne pepper (optional)
- Salt and pepper to taste
- 1 can (14 oz) diced tomatoes
- 1/4 cup chopped fresh parsley
- 1/4 cup chopped fresh mint
- Olive oil

Instructions:

1. Preheat your oven to 400°F (200°C).
2. Cut the eggplants in half lengthwise. Score the flesh of each half with a sharp knife in a crisscross pattern, being careful not to cut through the skin. Place the eggplant halves on a baking sheet, cut side up.
3. Drizzle the eggplant halves with olive oil and season with salt and pepper. Roast in the preheated oven for 20-25 minutes, or until the flesh is tender and golden brown.
4. While the eggplants are roasting, prepare the filling. Heat a drizzle of olive oil in a large skillet over medium heat. Add the chopped onion and cook until softened, about 5 minutes.
5. Add the minced garlic to the skillet and cook for another 1-2 minutes, until fragrant.
6. Add the ground lamb to the skillet, breaking it up with a spoon, and cook until browned and cooked through, about 5-7 minutes.

7. Stir in the pine nuts, ground cumin, ground coriander, ground cinnamon, cayenne pepper (if using), salt, and pepper. Cook for another 2-3 minutes, stirring occasionally.
8. Add the diced tomatoes to the skillet, along with their juices. Bring the mixture to a simmer and cook for 5-7 minutes, allowing the flavors to meld together.
9. Remove the skillet from the heat and stir in the chopped fresh parsley and chopped fresh mint.
10. Once the eggplants are roasted, remove them from the oven. Using a spoon, carefully scoop out some of the flesh from each eggplant half to create a cavity for the filling.
11. Spoon the lamb and pine nut filling into each eggplant half, pressing gently to pack it in.
12. Return the stuffed eggplants to the oven and bake for another 15-20 minutes, or until the filling is heated through and the eggplants are tender.
13. Serve the stuffed eggplants hot, garnished with additional chopped fresh parsley or mint if desired.

Enjoy the delicious and hearty stuffed eggplant with lamb and pine nuts as a satisfying main dish! It's perfect for a special dinner or any time you're craving a flavorful and comforting meal.

Spinach and feta borekas

Ingredients:

For the filling:

- 2 tablespoons olive oil
- 1 small onion, finely chopped
- 2 cloves garlic, minced
- 1 lb fresh spinach, washed and chopped
- Salt and pepper to taste
- 1/2 teaspoon ground nutmeg
- 1 cup crumbled feta cheese
- 1/4 cup grated Parmesan cheese
- 1 egg, beaten (for egg wash)

For the dough:

- 1 lb puff pastry dough, thawed if frozen
- Flour (for dusting)

Instructions:

1. Preheat your oven to 375°F (190°C). Line a baking sheet with parchment paper or lightly grease it with oil.
2. Heat the olive oil in a large skillet over medium heat. Add the chopped onion and minced garlic, and cook until softened, about 2-3 minutes.
3. Add the chopped spinach to the skillet and cook until wilted, stirring occasionally, about 3-4 minutes. Season with salt, pepper, and ground nutmeg.
4. Once the spinach is cooked, remove the skillet from the heat and let the mixture cool slightly.
5. Transfer the spinach mixture to a mixing bowl. Stir in the crumbled feta cheese and grated Parmesan cheese until well combined. Set aside.
6. Roll out the puff pastry dough on a lightly floured surface to about 1/8-inch thickness. Using a sharp knife or pizza cutter, cut the dough into squares, about 3-4 inches in size.

7. Place a spoonful of the spinach and feta filling in the center of each dough square.
8. Fold one corner of each dough square over the filling to meet the opposite corner, forming a triangle. Press the edges together firmly to seal.
9. Transfer the filled borekas to the prepared baking sheet, leaving space between each one.
10. Brush the tops of the borekas with beaten egg wash.
11. Bake in the preheated oven for 15-20 minutes, or until the borekas are golden brown and puffed up.
12. Remove the borekas from the oven and let them cool slightly before serving.

Enjoy the delicious spinach and feta borekas warm or at room temperature as a delightful snack or appetizer! They're perfect for parties, gatherings, or simply as a tasty treat any time of day.

Israeli beef stew with potatoes and carrots

Ingredients:

- 2 lbs beef stew meat, cut into cubes
- 2 tablespoons olive oil
- 1 onion, chopped
- 3 cloves garlic, minced
- 4 medium potatoes, peeled and cut into chunks
- 4 carrots, peeled and cut into chunks
- 1/4 cup tomato paste
- 4 cups beef broth
- 1 cup red wine (optional)
- 2 bay leaves
- 1 teaspoon dried thyme
- 1 teaspoon paprika
- Salt and pepper to taste
- Chopped fresh parsley for garnish (optional)

Instructions:

1. Preheat your oven to 300°F (150°C).
2. In a large oven-safe Dutch oven or heavy-bottomed pot, heat the olive oil over medium heat.
3. Add the chopped onion to the pot and cook until softened, about 5 minutes.
4. Add the minced garlic to the pot and cook for another 1-2 minutes, until fragrant.
5. Add the beef stew meat to the pot and brown on all sides, about 5-7 minutes.
6. Stir in the tomato paste, dried thyme, paprika, salt, and pepper, and cook for another 2 minutes.
7. Add the beef broth, red wine (if using), bay leaves, potatoes, and carrots to the pot. Bring the mixture to a simmer.
8. Once simmering, cover the pot with a lid and transfer it to the preheated oven.
9. Bake the stew in the oven for 2-3 hours, or until the beef is tender and the potatoes and carrots are cooked through.
10. Once cooked, remove the pot from the oven and discard the bay leaves.
11. Taste the stew and adjust the seasoning if needed, adding more salt and pepper as desired.

12. Serve the Israeli beef stew hot, garnished with chopped fresh parsley if desired.

Enjoy the delicious and comforting Israeli beef stew with potatoes and carrots as a satisfying meal for lunch or dinner! Serve it with crusty bread or over cooked rice for a complete and hearty dish.

Grilled za'atar chicken skewers

Ingredients:

- 1 lb boneless, skinless chicken breasts or thighs, cut into cubes
- 2 tablespoons olive oil
- 2 tablespoons za'atar seasoning
- 2 cloves garlic, minced
- Juice of 1 lemon
- Salt and pepper to taste
- Wooden skewers, soaked in water for at least 30 minutes

Instructions:

1. In a mixing bowl, combine the olive oil, za'atar seasoning, minced garlic, lemon juice, salt, and pepper. Stir until well combined.
2. Add the cubed chicken to the bowl with the marinade. Toss the chicken until evenly coated with the marinade. Cover the bowl and refrigerate for at least 30 minutes, or up to overnight, to allow the flavors to meld together.
3. Preheat your grill to medium-high heat. If using a grill pan indoors, heat it over medium-high heat on the stovetop.
4. While the grill is heating up, thread the marinated chicken cubes onto the soaked wooden skewers, leaving a little space between each piece.
5. Once the grill is hot, lightly oil the grates to prevent sticking. Place the chicken skewers on the grill and cook for 4-5 minutes per side, or until the chicken is cooked through and has nice grill marks.
6. While grilling, baste the chicken skewers with any remaining marinade to keep them moist and flavorful.
7. Once the chicken is cooked through, remove the skewers from the grill and transfer them to a serving platter.
8. Serve the grilled za'atar chicken skewers hot, garnished with lemon wedges and fresh herbs if desired.

Enjoy the delicious and aromatic grilled za'atar chicken skewers as a flavorful main dish for lunch or dinner! Serve them with your favorite sides, such as rice, grilled vegetables, or a fresh salad, for a complete and satisfying meal.

Mediterranean stuffed zucchini

Ingredients:

- 4 medium zucchini
- 1 tablespoon olive oil
- 1 small onion, finely chopped
- 2 cloves garlic, minced
- 1 red bell pepper, diced
- 1 yellow bell pepper, diced
- 1 cup cooked quinoa or rice
- 1 cup canned chickpeas, drained and rinsed
- 1 cup cherry tomatoes, halved
- 1/4 cup chopped fresh parsley
- 1/4 cup chopped fresh mint
- 1/2 cup crumbled feta cheese
- Salt and pepper to taste
- 1/4 teaspoon paprika
- Lemon wedges for serving
- Optional: Pine nuts or chopped almonds for garnish

Instructions:

1. Preheat your oven to 375°F (190°C). Lightly grease a baking dish with olive oil.
2. Cut each zucchini in half lengthwise. Use a spoon to carefully scoop out the flesh from the center of each zucchini half, leaving about a 1/4-inch border around the edges. Reserve the scooped-out zucchini flesh for later use.
3. Place the hollowed-out zucchini halves in the prepared baking dish, cut side up.
4. Heat the olive oil in a large skillet over medium heat. Add the chopped onion and cook until softened, about 5 minutes.
5. Add the minced garlic to the skillet and cook for another 1-2 minutes, until fragrant.
6. Add the diced red and yellow bell peppers to the skillet and cook for 3-4 minutes, until softened.
7. Chop the reserved zucchini flesh and add it to the skillet. Cook for another 3-4 minutes, until the zucchini is tender.

8. Remove the skillet from the heat and transfer the cooked vegetables to a large mixing bowl.
9. To the mixing bowl, add the cooked quinoa or rice, drained and rinsed chickpeas, halved cherry tomatoes, chopped fresh parsley, chopped fresh mint, and crumbled feta cheese. Season with salt, pepper, and paprika, and stir until well combined.
10. Spoon the filling mixture into the hollowed-out zucchini halves, pressing down gently to pack it in.
11. Cover the baking dish with foil and bake in the preheated oven for 25-30 minutes, or until the zucchini is tender and the filling is heated through.
12. Remove the foil from the baking dish and switch the oven to broil. Broil the stuffed zucchini for an additional 2-3 minutes, or until the tops are golden brown and slightly crispy.
13. Remove the stuffed zucchini from the oven and let them cool for a few minutes before serving.
14. Serve the Mediterranean stuffed zucchini hot, garnished with lemon wedges and optional pine nuts or chopped almonds for extra crunch.

Enjoy the flavorful and nutritious Mediterranean stuffed zucchini as a delicious vegetarian main dish or side dish! It's packed with vibrant colors and flavors that will delight your taste buds.

Spiced lamb burgers with yogurt sauce

Ingredients:

For the lamb burgers:

- 1 lb ground lamb
- 1/2 onion, finely chopped
- 2 cloves garlic, minced
- 2 tablespoons chopped fresh parsley
- 1 teaspoon ground cumin
- 1 teaspoon ground coriander
- 1/2 teaspoon ground paprika
- 1/2 teaspoon ground cinnamon
- 1/4 teaspoon cayenne pepper (optional, for extra heat)
- Salt and pepper to taste
- Olive oil, for cooking
- Burger buns, lettuce, tomato slices, and other toppings for serving

For the yogurt sauce:

- 1/2 cup Greek yogurt
- 1 tablespoon lemon juice
- 1 tablespoon chopped fresh mint or parsley
- 1 clove garlic, minced
- Salt and pepper to taste

Instructions:

1. In a large mixing bowl, combine the ground lamb, finely chopped onion, minced garlic, chopped fresh parsley, ground cumin, ground coriander, ground paprika, ground cinnamon, cayenne pepper (if using), salt, and pepper. Use your hands to mix everything together until well combined.
2. Divide the lamb mixture into 4 equal portions. Shape each portion into a patty, about 1/2 to 3/4 inch thick. Press a slight indentation into the center of each patty with your thumb to prevent them from puffing up during cooking.

3. Heat a grill pan or outdoor grill over medium-high heat. Brush the grill pan or grill grates with olive oil to prevent sticking.
4. Place the lamb patties on the preheated grill pan or grill. Cook for 4-5 minutes per side, or until the burgers are cooked to your desired doneness and have nice grill marks on both sides.
5. While the burgers are cooking, prepare the yogurt sauce. In a small bowl, combine the Greek yogurt, lemon juice, chopped fresh mint or parsley, minced garlic, salt, and pepper. Stir until well mixed. Adjust the seasoning to taste.
6. Once the lamb burgers are cooked, remove them from the grill and let them rest for a few minutes.
7. Toast the burger buns on the grill, if desired.
8. To assemble the burgers, place a lamb patty on the bottom half of each burger bun. Top with a dollop of yogurt sauce and any desired toppings such as lettuce, tomato slices, and onion slices. Place the top half of the burger bun over the toppings.
9. Serve the spiced lamb burgers with yogurt sauce immediately, and enjoy!

These spiced lamb burgers with yogurt sauce are full of flavor and make a delicious and satisfying meal. Serve them at your next barbecue or weeknight dinner for a tasty twist on classic burgers.

Herb-crusted salmon

Ingredients:

- 4 salmon fillets, skin-on or skinless, about 6 ounces each
- 2 tablespoons Dijon mustard
- 2 tablespoons olive oil
- 2 cloves garlic, minced
- 1 tablespoon chopped fresh parsley
- 1 tablespoon chopped fresh dill
- 1 tablespoon chopped fresh chives
- 1 teaspoon chopped fresh thyme (optional)
- Salt and pepper to taste
- Lemon wedges for serving

Instructions:

1. Preheat your oven to 400°F (200°C). Line a baking sheet with parchment paper or lightly grease it with olive oil.
2. In a small bowl, mix together the Dijon mustard, olive oil, minced garlic, chopped fresh parsley, chopped fresh dill, chopped fresh chives, chopped fresh thyme (if using), salt, and pepper.
3. Place the salmon fillets on the prepared baking sheet, skin-side down if using skin-on fillets.
4. Spoon the herb mixture evenly over the top of each salmon fillet, spreading it out with the back of a spoon to coat the entire surface.
5. Bake the herb-crusted salmon in the preheated oven for 12-15 minutes, or until the salmon is cooked through and flakes easily with a fork.
6. If desired, switch the oven to broil for the last 1-2 minutes of cooking to crisp up the herb crust.
7. Remove the salmon from the oven and let it rest for a few minutes before serving.
8. Serve the herb-crusted salmon hot, garnished with lemon wedges for squeezing over the top.

Enjoy the flavorful and tender herb-crusted salmon as a delicious main dish! Serve it with your favorite sides, such as roasted vegetables, steamed rice, or a fresh salad, for a complete and satisfying meal.

Israeli-style ratatouille

Ingredients:

- 2 medium eggplants, diced
- 2 zucchinis, diced
- 2 bell peppers (red, yellow, or orange), diced
- 2 onions, diced
- 4 cloves garlic, minced
- 4 ripe tomatoes, diced
- 2 tablespoons tomato paste
- 2 teaspoons paprika
- 1 teaspoon ground cumin
- 1 teaspoon ground coriander
- 1/2 teaspoon ground turmeric
- 1/2 teaspoon red pepper flakes (optional, for heat)
- Salt and pepper to taste
- Olive oil
- Fresh parsley or cilantro for garnish

Instructions:

1. Heat a couple of tablespoons of olive oil in a large skillet or Dutch oven over medium heat.
2. Add the diced onions to the skillet and cook until softened, about 5 minutes.
3. Add the minced garlic to the skillet and cook for another 1-2 minutes, until fragrant.
4. Add the diced eggplants to the skillet and cook for 5-7 minutes, stirring occasionally, until they start to soften.
5. Add the diced zucchinis and bell peppers to the skillet and cook for another 5 minutes, until they begin to soften.
6. Stir in the diced tomatoes, tomato paste, paprika, ground cumin, ground coriander, ground turmeric, red pepper flakes (if using), salt, and pepper. Mix well to combine.
7. Reduce the heat to low, cover the skillet, and let the ratatouille simmer for 20-25 minutes, stirring occasionally, until all the vegetables are tender and the flavors have melded together.

8. Taste the ratatouille and adjust the seasoning if needed, adding more salt and pepper to taste.
9. Once cooked, remove the skillet from the heat and let the ratatouille cool slightly.
10. Serve the Israeli-style ratatouille hot, garnished with fresh parsley or cilantro.

Israeli-style ratatouille is delicious on its own as a vegetarian main dish or served as a side dish alongside grilled meats or fish. Enjoy its vibrant flavors and hearty texture!

Harissa roasted vegetables

Ingredients:

- Assorted vegetables, such as:
    - 2 bell peppers (red, yellow, or orange), cut into chunks
    - 1 eggplant, cut into cubes
    - 2 zucchinis, sliced
    - 1 red onion, cut into wedges
    - 1 cup cherry tomatoes
- 2 tablespoons harissa paste
- 2 tablespoons olive oil
- 2 cloves garlic, minced
- 1 teaspoon ground cumin
- 1 teaspoon ground coriander
- 1/2 teaspoon smoked paprika
- Salt and pepper to taste
- Fresh parsley or cilantro for garnish (optional)

Instructions:

1. Preheat your oven to 400°F (200°C). Line a baking sheet with parchment paper or lightly grease it with olive oil.
2. In a small bowl, mix together the harissa paste, olive oil, minced garlic, ground cumin, ground coriander, smoked paprika, salt, and pepper.
3. In a large mixing bowl, toss the assorted vegetables with the harissa mixture until evenly coated.
4. Spread the vegetables out in a single layer on the prepared baking sheet.
5. Roast the vegetables in the preheated oven for 25-30 minutes, stirring halfway through, or until they are tender and caramelized around the edges.
6. Once roasted, remove the vegetables from the oven and transfer them to a serving platter.
7. Garnish the harissa roasted vegetables with fresh parsley or cilantro, if desired.
8. Serve the vegetables hot as a flavorful side dish or vegetarian main course.

Enjoy the delicious and aromatic flavors of harissa roasted vegetables! They make a colorful and nutritious addition to any meal, and the spicy kick of harissa adds an extra layer of flavor that's sure to please your taste buds.

Beef and eggplant moussaka

Ingredients:

For the eggplant layer:

- 2 large eggplants, sliced into 1/4-inch rounds
- Salt
- Olive oil for brushing

For the beef layer:

- 1 lb ground beef
- 1 onion, finely chopped
- 3 cloves garlic, minced
- 1 can (14 oz) diced tomatoes
- 2 tablespoons tomato paste
- 1 teaspoon dried oregano
- 1/2 teaspoon ground cinnamon
- Salt and pepper to taste

For the béchamel sauce:

- 4 tablespoons unsalted butter
- 1/4 cup all-purpose flour
- 2 cups milk
- 1/4 teaspoon ground nutmeg
- Salt and pepper to taste
- 2 large eggs, beaten

Instructions:

1. Preheat your oven to 400°F (200°C). Lightly grease a large baking dish with olive oil.

2. Place the sliced eggplant rounds in a colander and sprinkle them liberally with salt. Let them sit for about 30 minutes to release excess moisture. Pat the eggplant slices dry with paper towels.
3. Arrange the eggplant slices on a baking sheet in a single layer. Brush both sides of the eggplant slices with olive oil. Roast in the preheated oven for 20-25 minutes, flipping halfway through, until softened and lightly browned. Remove from the oven and set aside.
4. While the eggplant is roasting, prepare the beef layer. In a large skillet, heat a tablespoon of olive oil over medium heat. Add the chopped onion and cook until softened, about 5 minutes. Add the minced garlic and cook for another minute.
5. Add the ground beef to the skillet and cook until browned, breaking it up with a spoon as it cooks. Drain any excess fat from the skillet.
6. Stir in the diced tomatoes, tomato paste, dried oregano, ground cinnamon, salt, and pepper. Simmer the mixture for about 10 minutes, until the flavors meld together and the sauce thickens slightly. Remove from heat and set aside.
7. To make the béchamel sauce, melt the butter in a medium saucepan over medium heat. Once melted, whisk in the flour and cook for 1-2 minutes, until bubbly and golden brown.
8. Gradually whisk in the milk, stirring constantly to prevent lumps from forming. Cook the sauce, stirring frequently, until it thickens enough to coat the back of a spoon.
9. Remove the saucepan from the heat and stir in the ground nutmeg, salt, and pepper. Allow the sauce to cool slightly.
10. Once the sauce has cooled slightly, gradually whisk in the beaten eggs until smooth and creamy. Set aside.
11. To assemble the moussaka, spread half of the beef mixture in the bottom of the prepared baking dish. Arrange half of the roasted eggplant slices on top of the beef layer.
12. Repeat with another layer of the remaining beef mixture and eggplant slices.
13. Pour the béchamel sauce evenly over the top of the assembled moussaka, spreading it out with a spatula to cover the entire surface.
14. Reduce the oven temperature to 375°F (190°C). Bake the moussaka in the preheated oven for 40-45 minutes, or until the top is golden brown and bubbly.
15. Remove the moussaka from the oven and let it cool for 10-15 minutes before slicing and serving.
16. Serve the beef and eggplant moussaka warm, garnished with fresh herbs if desired.

Enjoy the rich and comforting flavors of beef and eggplant moussaka! It's a hearty and satisfying dish that's perfect for a cozy dinner or special occasion.

Chicken and vegetable kebabs with sumac

Ingredients:

- 1 lb boneless, skinless chicken breasts or thighs, cut into chunks
- 2 bell peppers (red, yellow, or orange), cut into chunks
- 1 red onion, cut into chunks
- 1 zucchini, sliced into rounds
- 8-10 cherry tomatoes
- 2 tablespoons olive oil
- 2 cloves garlic, minced
- 1 tablespoon sumac
- 1 teaspoon ground cumin
- 1 teaspoon paprika
- Salt and pepper to taste
- Wooden or metal skewers

Instructions:

1. If using wooden skewers, soak them in water for at least 30 minutes to prevent them from burning during grilling.
2. In a large mixing bowl, combine the olive oil, minced garlic, sumac, ground cumin, paprika, salt, and pepper. Mix well to combine.
3. Add the chicken chunks to the bowl with the marinade and toss until evenly coated. Cover the bowl and refrigerate for at least 30 minutes to allow the flavors to meld together.
4. Preheat your grill to medium-high heat. If using a grill pan indoors, heat it over medium-high heat on the stovetop.
5. While the grill is heating up, prepare the vegetable skewers. Thread the marinated chicken chunks, bell pepper chunks, red onion chunks, zucchini slices, and cherry tomatoes onto the skewers, alternating between the different ingredients.
6. Brush the grill grates with oil to prevent sticking. Place the assembled skewers on the preheated grill.
7. Grill the chicken and vegetable skewers for 8-10 minutes, turning occasionally, or until the chicken is cooked through and the vegetables are tender and slightly charred.

8. Once cooked, remove the skewers from the grill and let them rest for a few minutes.
9. Serve the chicken and vegetable kebabs with sumac hot, garnished with fresh herbs if desired.

Enjoy the flavorful and colorful chicken and vegetable kebabs with sumac as a delicious main dish for lunch or dinner! Serve them with rice, couscous, or pita bread and a side of tzatziki sauce or hummus for a complete and satisfying meal.

Lamb shawarma bowl

Ingredients:

For the lamb shawarma:

- 1 lb lamb shoulder, thinly sliced
- 2 tablespoons olive oil
- 2 cloves garlic, minced
- 1 teaspoon ground cumin
- 1 teaspoon ground coriander
- 1 teaspoon smoked paprika
- 1/2 teaspoon ground turmeric
- 1/2 teaspoon ground cinnamon
- 1/4 teaspoon cayenne pepper (optional, for heat)
- Salt and pepper to taste
- Juice of 1 lemon
- 2 tablespoons plain Greek yogurt

For the bowl:

- Cooked rice, quinoa, or couscous
- Mixed salad greens or shredded lettuce
- Sliced cucumber
- Sliced tomatoes
- Sliced red onion
- Kalamata olives
- Hummus
- Tzatziki sauce or tahini sauce
- Fresh parsley or cilantro for garnish
- Pita bread or flatbread (optional)

Instructions:

1. In a large mixing bowl, combine the olive oil, minced garlic, ground cumin, ground coriander, smoked paprika, ground turmeric, ground cinnamon, cayenne pepper (if using), salt, pepper, lemon juice, and Greek yogurt. Mix well to combine.
2. Add the thinly sliced lamb shoulder to the bowl with the marinade and toss until evenly coated. Cover the bowl and refrigerate for at least 1 hour, or preferably overnight, to allow the flavors to meld together.
3. Preheat your grill or grill pan over medium-high heat. If using a grill pan, lightly oil the surface to prevent sticking.
4. Thread the marinated lamb slices onto skewers or place them directly on the grill. Cook for 3-4 minutes per side, or until the lamb is cooked through and has nice grill marks.
5. Once cooked, remove the lamb from the grill and let it rest for a few minutes. Then, thinly slice the lamb into strips.
6. To assemble the shawarma bowls, start by placing a serving of cooked rice, quinoa, or couscous in each bowl.
7. Top the grains with mixed salad greens or shredded lettuce, sliced cucumber, sliced tomatoes, sliced red onion, and Kalamata olives.
8. Add the sliced lamb shawarma on top of the vegetables.
9. Serve the lamb shawarma bowls with hummus, tzatziki sauce or tahini sauce drizzled over the top.
10. Garnish with fresh parsley or cilantro.
11. Serve the lamb shawarma bowls hot, with pita bread or flatbread on the side if desired.

Enjoy the flavorful and satisfying lamb shawarma bowl as a delicious and nutritious meal! It's perfect for lunch or dinner and can be customized with your favorite toppings and sauces.

Spicy tomato and pepper soup

Ingredients:

- 2 tablespoons olive oil
- 1 onion, chopped
- 2 cloves garlic, minced
- 2 red bell peppers, chopped
- 2 yellow bell peppers, chopped
- 1 can (28 oz) diced tomatoes
- 4 cups vegetable or chicken broth
- 1 teaspoon smoked paprika
- 1/2 teaspoon ground cumin
- 1/2 teaspoon chili powder
- Salt and pepper to taste
- Fresh basil or cilantro for garnish (optional)
- Red pepper flakes for extra heat (optional)

Instructions:

1. Heat the olive oil in a large pot over medium heat. Add the chopped onion and cook until softened, about 5 minutes.
2. Add the minced garlic to the pot and cook for another minute, until fragrant.
3. Add the chopped red and yellow bell peppers to the pot and cook for 5-7 minutes, until they begin to soften.
4. Stir in the diced tomatoes (with their juices) and vegetable or chicken broth. Bring the mixture to a simmer.
5. Once simmering, add the smoked paprika, ground cumin, chili powder, salt, and pepper to the pot. Stir well to combine.
6. Let the soup simmer for 20-25 minutes, stirring occasionally, until the vegetables are tender and the flavors have melded together.
7. Taste the soup and adjust the seasoning if needed, adding more salt, pepper, or spices to taste. If you like your soup extra spicy, you can add red pepper flakes at this point.
8. Once the soup is ready, remove it from the heat and let it cool slightly.
9. Using an immersion blender or countertop blender, puree the soup until smooth and creamy. Be careful when blending hot liquids.

10. Return the blended soup to the pot and reheat gently over low heat if necessary.
11. Serve the spicy tomato and pepper soup hot, garnished with fresh basil or cilantro if desired.

Enjoy the flavorful and warming spicy tomato and pepper soup as a comforting meal on a chilly day! Serve it with crusty bread or a side salad for a complete and satisfying dish.

Baked falafel with tahini dressing

Ingredients:

For the baked falafel:

- 2 cans (15 oz each) chickpeas, drained and rinsed
- 1 small onion, chopped
- 3 cloves garlic, minced
- 1/4 cup chopped fresh parsley
- 1/4 cup chopped fresh cilantro
- 2 tablespoons olive oil
- 2 tablespoons lemon juice
- 1 teaspoon ground cumin
- 1 teaspoon ground coriander
- 1/2 teaspoon baking soda
- Salt and pepper to taste

For the tahini dressing:

- 1/4 cup tahini paste
- 2 tablespoons lemon juice
- 2 tablespoons water
- 1 clove garlic, minced
- Salt to taste

For serving:

- Pita bread or wraps
- Lettuce, sliced tomatoes, sliced cucumbers, sliced red onions (optional)
- Additional tahini dressing for drizzling

Instructions:

1. Preheat your oven to 375°F (190°C). Line a baking sheet with parchment paper or lightly grease it with olive oil.
2. In a food processor, combine the drained and rinsed chickpeas, chopped onion, minced garlic, chopped fresh parsley, chopped fresh cilantro, olive oil, lemon juice, ground cumin, ground coriander, baking soda, salt, and pepper. Pulse until the mixture comes together but still has some texture. Avoid over-processing; you want the mixture to be slightly chunky.
3. Using your hands, shape the falafel mixture into small balls or patties, about 1 1/2 inches in diameter. Place them on the prepared baking sheet.
4. Bake the falafel in the preheated oven for 20-25 minutes, flipping halfway through, until they are golden brown and crispy on the outside.
5. While the falafel is baking, prepare the tahini dressing. In a small bowl, whisk together the tahini paste, lemon juice, water, minced garlic, and salt until smooth and creamy. Adjust the consistency with more water if needed.
6. Once the falafel is baked, remove them from the oven and let them cool slightly.
7. Serve the baked falafel warm, stuffed into pita bread or wraps along with lettuce, sliced tomatoes, sliced cucumbers, sliced red onions, if desired. Drizzle with tahini dressing before serving.
8. Enjoy the baked falafel with tahini dressing as a delicious and satisfying meal!

This baked falafel with tahini dressing is packed with flavor and makes a nutritious and satisfying dish. It's perfect for lunch or dinner and can be customized with your favorite toppings and additions.

Israeli-style stuffed cabbage rolls

Ingredients:

For the cabbage rolls:

- 1 large head of green cabbage
- 1 cup long-grain rice, rinsed and drained
- 1 lb ground beef or lamb
- 1 onion, finely chopped
- 3 cloves garlic, minced
- 1/4 cup chopped fresh parsley
- 1/4 cup chopped fresh dill
- Salt and pepper to taste
- 1/2 teaspoon ground cumin
- 1/2 teaspoon ground cinnamon
- 1/4 teaspoon ground allspice
- 1/4 teaspoon ground nutmeg

For the tomato sauce:

- 1 can (28 oz) crushed tomatoes
- 2 cups vegetable or beef broth
- 2 tablespoons tomato paste
- 2 tablespoons olive oil
- 2 cloves garlic, minced
- 1 teaspoon paprika
- Salt and pepper to taste

Instructions:

1. Bring a large pot of water to a boil. Carefully remove the core from the cabbage and place the whole head of cabbage in the boiling water. Cook for 3-4 minutes, or until the outer leaves are softened and can be easily peeled away. Remove the cabbage from the pot and let it cool slightly. Repeat the process until you have enough softened cabbage leaves to make the desired number of rolls.

2. In a large mixing bowl, combine the rinsed and drained rice, ground beef or lamb, finely chopped onion, minced garlic, chopped fresh parsley, chopped fresh dill, salt, pepper, ground cumin, ground cinnamon, ground allspice, and ground nutmeg. Mix well to combine.
3. Place a cabbage leaf on a flat surface and trim off the tough rib at the base of the leaf. Spoon a small amount of the filling mixture onto the center of the leaf and fold the sides over the filling. Roll up the leaf tightly to form a cabbage roll. Repeat with the remaining cabbage leaves and filling mixture.
4. To make the tomato sauce, heat the olive oil in a large skillet or Dutch oven over medium heat. Add the minced garlic and cook for 1-2 minutes, until fragrant. Stir in the crushed tomatoes, vegetable or beef broth, tomato paste, paprika, salt, and pepper. Bring the sauce to a simmer.
5. Carefully place the cabbage rolls seam-side down in the simmering tomato sauce. Spoon some of the sauce over the top of the cabbage rolls.
6. Cover the skillet or Dutch oven with a lid and simmer the cabbage rolls over low heat for 45-50 minutes, or until the rice is cooked through and the cabbage is tender.
7. Once cooked, remove the cabbage rolls from the sauce and transfer them to a serving platter.
8. Serve the Israeli-style stuffed cabbage rolls hot, garnished with additional chopped fresh dill or parsley if desired. Serve the extra tomato sauce on the side.

Enjoy the flavorful and comforting Israeli-style stuffed cabbage rolls as a satisfying main dish! They pair well with crusty bread or a simple salad for a complete and delicious meal.

www.ingramcontent.com/pod-product-compliance
Lightning Source LLC
LaVergne TN
LVHW081602060526
838201LV00054B/2039